Poison Ivy

This weed (above) causes an itchy
rash if you touch it. Poison ivy grows
as a vine or shrub. Try to remember
what the leaves look like, and do
not touch them or other parts of
the plant. If you do touch poison
ivy, washing your hands as soon as
possible may reduce the itching.
Your local drugstore will have
various remedies that will help.

World Book's

SCIENCE
& NATURE
GUIDES

FRESHWATER
LIFE

OF THE UNITED STATES AND CANADA

World Book, Inc.
a Scott Fetzer company
Chicago

Scientific names

In this book, after the common name of an organism (life form) is given, that organism's scientific name usually appears. Scientific names are put into a special type of lettering, called italic, *which looks like this.*

The first name in a scientific name is the genus. A genus consists of very similar groups, but the members of these different groups usually cannot breed with one another. The second name given is the species. Every known organism belongs to a particular species. Members of the same species can breed with one another, and the young grow up to look very much like their parents.

Therefore, when you see a name like *Nerodia taxispilota,* you know that the genus is *Nerodia* and the species is *taxispilota. Nerodia taxispilota* is the scientific name for the brown water snake (see page 10). An animal's scientific name is the same worldwide. This helps scientists and students to know which animal is being discussed, since the animal may have many different common names. The abbreviation "spp." after a genus name indicates that a group of species from the genus is being discussed.

Some animals in this book are really representative of a larger group than just a genus. For instance, there are thousands of species of copepods (see page 36) that are all fairly similar. For such animals, the group—for example, the family, class, or order—that the animal typifies is given instead of a genus name. Groupings such as classes or orders are not put into italic type.

Countryside Code

1 **Always go collecting with a friend,** and always tell an adult where you are going.
2 **Leave animal nests or dens untouched.**
3 **Keep clear of any wild animals that you find**—they may attack you if frightened.
4 **Keep to existing roads, trails, and pathways** wherever possible.

This edition published in the United States of America by World Book, Inc., Chicago.

WORLD BOOK and the GLOBE DEVICE are registered trademarks or trademarks of World Book, Inc.

World Book, Inc.
233 North Michigan Avenue
Chicago, IL 60601 USA

For information about other World Book publications, visit our Web site **http://www.worldbook.com,** or call **1-800-WORLDBK (967-5325).** For information about sales to schools and libraries, call **1-800-975-3250 (United States); 1-800-837-5365 (Canada).**

Library of Congress Cataloging-in-Publication Data

Freshwater life of the United States and Canada.
  p. cm. —(World Book's science & nature guides)
  Includes bibliographical references (p.).
  ISBN 0-7166-4213-1 — ISBN 0-7166-4208-5 (set)
    1. Freshwater animals—United States—Juvenile literature.
  2. Freshwater Animals—Canada—Juvenile literature. I. World Book, Inc. II. Series.

  QL155 .F74 2005
  591.76'097—dc22
                                                    2004043484

Habitat paintings by Mike Saunders; headbands by Antonia Phillips; identification and activities illustrations by Mr. Gay Galsworthy.

For World Book:
General Managing Editor: Paul A. Kobasa
Editorial: Shawn Brennan, Maureen Liebenson, Christine Sullivan
Research: Madolynn Cronk, Lynn Durbin, Cheryl Graham, Karen McCormack, Loranne Shields, Hilary Zawidowski
Librarian: Jon Fjortoft
Permissions: Janet Peterson
Graphics and Design: Sandra Dyrlund, Anne Fritzinger
Indexing: Aamir Burki, David Pofelski
Pre-press and Manufacturing: Carma Fazio, Steve Hueppchen, Jared Svoboda, Madelyn Underwood
Text Processing: Curley Hunter, Gwendolyn Johnson
Proofreading: Anne Dillon

Printed in China
1 2 3 4 5 6 7 8 9 10 09 08 07 06 05 04

Contents

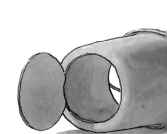

Entries *like this*
indicate pages
featuring projects
you can do!

Introduction To Freshwater Life

From quiet ponds and peaceful lakes to rushing mountain streams and steaming swamps, you can see freshwater areas are alive with animals. Water reptiles—turtles, for instance—and amphibians—such as frogs—spend part of their time on land and part in the water. These types of animals have lungs and must come to the water's surface to breathe.

Some water snails have simple lungs and live in still ponds, where there is not much oxygen. Many insects start life in the water before changing into adults that live on land. But most other water animals, such as fish, breathe using gills and will soon die if taken out of the water. This book will make it easier for you to identify freshwater creatures by grouping them according to the habitat, or type of freshwater environment, where you are most likely to see them. Remember that many animals may be found in more than one habitat.

Body-changing insects

Some freshwater creatures undergo a change of form as they mature, which is called metamorphosis. Dragonflies begin their lives as eggs laid in water or on a water plant by an adult female. The eggs hatch into larvae called nymphs, which then live underwater for several years, hiding among the plants and catching other animals for food.

Eventually, the nymphs crawl out of the water and become adult dragonflies—they then have wings and are no longer adapted for living in the water. Their gills are replaced by lungs, which cannot extract oxygen from water. Stoneflies, Mayflies, alderflies, and damsel flies have similar patterns of development.

The eggs hatch into larvae (young insects), which are known as nymphs.

The adult dragonflies mate over water, and the female then lays her eggs in water or on a water plant.

Each nymph has gills that permit it to breathe underwater. The nymphs are ferocious hunters and attack anything in sight, including small fish.

Nymphs molt (shed their old skin) about 12 times as they grow under the water.

How to use this book

To identify an animal that you don't recognize, such as the two animals shown here, follow these steps:

1. **Decide what habitat you are in.** If you're unsure about this, read the descriptions at the start of each section to see which one fits best. Each habitat has a different picture-band heading, shown at the bottom right of this page.

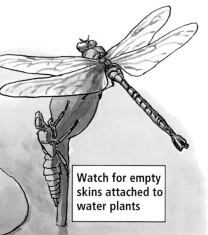

2. **Decide what sort of animal it is.** Is it a reptile or an amphibian, a fish or a mollusk, or something else entirely? Look at the descriptions on pages 6–7 to find out. For example, the freshwater shrimp (left) is a crustacean.

3. **Look through the pages for your animal under the picture-band for the habitat you are in.** The picture and information given for each animal can help you identify it.

4. **If you can't find the animal there,** look through the other sections. Animals move around, and you may see them in more than one habitat. You will find the frog (right) is a northern leopard frog (see page 13).

5. **If you still can't find the animal,** you may need to look in a larger field guide. You may have spotted a very rare creature!

Finally, the nymph crawls up a plant stem into the air and molts for a final time. Out crawls the adult dragonfly with its brightly colored body. After its wings dry, the insect flies away. The dragonfly is now a land-based insect.

Watch for empty skins attached to water plants

Top-of-page picture bands

This book is divided into different freshwater habitats. Each habitat (type of environment) has a different picture band at the top of the page. These are shown below.

Found Almost Everywhere

Ponds & Shallow Lakes

Swamps & Marshes

Deep & Cold Waters

Fast Streams & Rivers

Slow Rivers & Canals

What To Look For

Reptiles

Alligators, turtles, snakes, and lizards are all reptiles. (Lizards live on land and are not covered in this book.) Reptiles have skin covered in scales, or hard plates and shields. Excepting snakes, reptiles have claws on their toes.

Amphibians

Most frogs have smooth skin that is wet to the touch.

Toads have tough, bumpy skin that is dry to the touch.

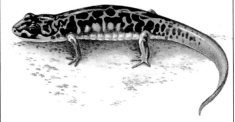

Salamanders have smooth, moist skin; most have stout front and back legs of equal size. The belly (underneath) may be a different color from the back.

Frogs, toads, newts, and salamanders are all amphibians. Their skin has no scales. They do not have claws on their toes. They lay jellylike eggs in water, which hatch into larvae or tadpoles.

Fish

It is usually easy to recognize a fish. (However, be careful not to mistake eels for amphiumas or sirens [see page 27]—the last two are both amphibians and have tiny legs.) Look for the number and position of the fins on the fish, especially those on the back, which are called the dorsal fins.

Eels have one long fin.

Sunfish have one long fin that is spiny in front and soft at the back.

Minnows have one short fin.

Perch and darters have two fins that are close together.

Trout have two fins, one large and one tiny.

Mollusks

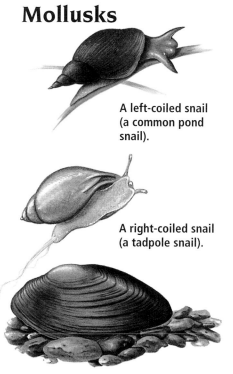

A left-coiled snail (a common pond snail).

A right-coiled snail (a tadpole snail).

A bivalve (a pearl mussel).

All mollusks are soft-bodied animals and most have a shell (sometimes called a valve). Animals with one shell are called gastropods. Those with two hinged shells are called bivalves. When you see a water snail, check whether its shell coils to the left or right. Hold the shell upright with the aperture (main opening) facing you and follow the coil with your finger.

Crustaceans

Crustaceans have a hard, plated shell, long feelers for finding food, and many pairs of jointed legs. As they grow, they must molt their shell and grow a bigger one. Crayfish, shrimps, and lobsters are all crustaceans.

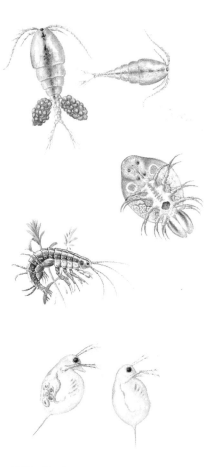

Insect larvae

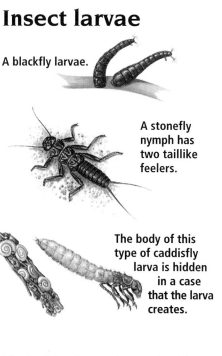

A blackfly larvae.

A stonefly nymph has two taillike feelers.

The body of this type of caddisfly larva is hidden in a case that the larva creates.

Most of the insect larvae in this book are nymphs. They have bodies that are divided into three parts: head, middle (thorax), and rear (abdomen). There are three pairs of jointed legs on the thorax. There are no legs on the abdomen, though some larvae have many pairs of feathery gills—try to count these.

A fly larva looks very different from a nymph. It has a small wormlike body divided into segments. Most fly larvae are legless.

Worms have no legs and no hard skin or shell. They are usually long and thin. Flatworms have flat, soft bodies and live on land or in water. Earthworms have round segmented bodies that give them a ringed appearance, and there is no obvious head. A leech's body is also divided into segments. The leech has suckers at both ends, but they are difficult to see.

Worms & wormlike animals

Found Almost Everywhere

Some water animals don't seem to mind where they live. They can be found in streams, rivers, ponds, lakes, or swamps. Many of these creatures also have a large range, or geographic area, in which they live. You may spot them throughout much of the United States and Canada. The picture shows animals from this book—see how many you can identify.

Reptiles

Western Aquatic Garter Snake
(Thamnophis couchii)

This snake can be hard to identify because it varies in color. It can have three stripes, or be spotted or blotched. Sometimes it has no back stripe at all. The aquatic garter snake lives mainly in rivers and streams, but it can also be found in coastal marshes and in mountain waters. This snake is active mainly during the day, when it feeds on fish, frogs, toads, salamanders, earthworms, and leeches. Instead of laying eggs, females of this group give birth to live young.
Group: Colubrid snakes—Size: 1½–5 ft (0.5–1.5 m)
Distribution: The western region of the U.S. into Mexico

Brown Water Snake
(Nerodia taxispilota)

As its common name would indicate, this heavy snake is brown or dark brown. It has three rows of big, dark blotches running down its back and sides and a yellow belly with dark spots. The brown water snake lives around rivers, lakes, and large ponds, often taking the sun on the banks or on tree branches that overhang the water. It is most active by day and feeds on frogs and fish. **Beware of this snake, as it is aggressive and gives a nasty bite.**

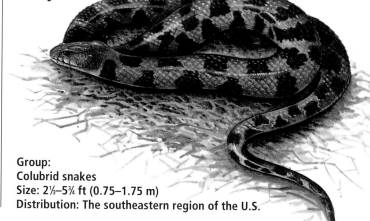

Group:
Colubrid snakes
Size: 2⅓–5¾ ft (0.75–1.75 m)
Distribution: The southeastern region of the U.S.

Northern Water Snake
(Nerodia sipedon)

This snake is brownish in color with dark bands in the neck area and squarish dark blotches on its back and sides. Its belly is white, yellow, or gray. This snake can be seen in most water habitats, such as lakes, ponds, rivers, ditches, and bogs. It hunts by day and by night, catching and eating frogs, salamanders, turtles, and small fish. During the day, it may also bask on rocks. The northern water snake is more likely to flee than attack, but if angry, it will strike with its body and bite. Unfortunately, water snakes are often mistaken for poisonous cottonmouths and are killed.
Group: Colubrid snakes—Size: nearly 2–4½ ft (0.6–1.4 m)
Distribution: Southeastern Canada and most of the eastern U.S.

Painted Turtle
(Chrysemys picta)

This little turtle gets its name from its brightly patterned shell, which looks as if it has been painted with red and yellow bars. The basic color of the shell is olive or black, and it is smooth and rather flattened. The painted turtle's neck, legs, and tail match its shell beautifully, as they are also patterned with red and yellow stripes. Painted turtles live in shallow streams, rivers, and lakes. They sunbathe on logs, often in big groups. Their favorite foods include crayfish, small mollusks, insects, and water plants. They are the most widespread turtle in North America.
Group: Pond and box turtles—Size: 4–10 in (10–25 cm)
Distribution: Southern Canada and most of the northern and eastern U.S.

Diamondback Water Snake
(Nerodia rhombifer)

So called because of the diamond pattern on its back, this snake is greenish-brown with black markings and a yellow belly. The diamondback water snake is active during the day, and it can often be spotted basking on logs along the edges of lakes, rivers, streams, or in swamps or ditches. It feeds on fish and frogs. **Be careful if you spot this snake, as it is aggressive and quick to bite.**
Group: Colubrid snakes
Size: 3–5¼ ft (1–1.6 m)
Distribution: The central U.S. from Illinois and Indiana, south through Mexico

Snapping Turtle
(Chelydra serpentina)

This aggressive turtle is one to keep away from. You will recognize it easily by its big, knobby head, hooked jaws, and a tail that is as long as its shell. The snapping turtle will snap at just about anything, including your fingers and toes! It eats plants and a great variety of live and dead animals. The shell is plain tan to dark brown; the edge of the shell is scalloped, with a more jagged pattern near the tail. The undershell is yellow to tan and quite small. You'll rarely see the snapping turtle out of water, not even to sunbathe on the riverbank. It prefers to rest in warm, muddy, shallow water, with only its snout visible, waiting for its next meal.

Group: Snapping turtles
Size: Up to 19 in (47 cm)
Distribution: All but the western regions of Canada and the U.S.

Amphibians

Found Almost Everywhere

American Toad
(Bufo americanus)

It can be difficult to tell the different species of toads apart, but it is easier to tell toads from frogs—unlike the smooth-skinned frog, the toad has a rough, bumpy skin. The large American toad can be brown, brick-red, or olive, with patterns in lighter colors. Warty-looking bumps on its tough hide are brown to orange-red, and there are large bony crests above its eyes. There may be a light stripe down the middle of its back, and its belly usually has spots. The American toad lives in a variety of places, from grassy backyards to mountains wherever there is enough moisture and enough insects for it to eat. It usually becomes most active at night. In the spring, listen then for the American toad's beautiful call.

Group: Toads
Size: 2–4½ in (6–11.5 cm)
Distribution: Widespread in eastern North America

Western Toad
(Bufo boreas)

This toad is large and green, gray, brown, or red in color, with a light stripe down the middle of its back. Bumps on its body are reddish and surrounded by black blotches. It has no crests above its eyes, which may help you to identify it. The western toad is found in various places, from desert streams and springs to woodlands, grasslands, and mountain meadows. You will see it walking rather than hopping. It makes burrows for itself or inhabits those of squirrels and other small mammals. Listen for the voice of the western toad at twilight—it sounds something like a chick chirping.

Group: Toads—Size: 2½–5 in (6.5–12.5 cm)
Distribution: Pacific coast of North America, and east to the Rocky Mts. and western regions of the U.S. and Canada

Mudpuppy
(Necturus maculosus)

Group: Mudpuppies and water dogs
Size: 8–17 in (20–42 cm)
Distribution: Most of eastern half of the U.S., excluding the coastal strip, and in the eastern central region of Canada

The mudpuppy, or waterdog, is a kind of salamander that remains a larva all its life. You can easily recognize the mudpuppy by the maroon gills around its neck, which look like a feathery collar. It is gray to rusty-brown in color, with faint, blue-black spots. The belly is gray with dark spots. It has four toes on each of its four feet. It lives in all kinds of ponds, lakes, rivers, and streams, especially those that are muddy and full of weeds. It feeds on fish eggs, crayfish, water insects, and mollusks.

Chorus Frog
(Pseudacris spp.)

You are more likely to hear this tree frog than see it. During the spring, it sings night and day in grassy areas near water, in woodlands, and in swamps, but it is always well hidden. The sound it makes is like the sound you get by running a fingernail over the teeth of a comb. The chorus frog has greenish-brown, smooth skin, with three dark, sometimes brown, stripes down the back. There is a dark stripe through its eye and a white stripe along its upper lip.

Group: Tree frogs
Size: ¾–1½ in (2–4 cm)
Distribution: Widespread over most of North America, except in the Pacific regions

Northern Leopard Frog
(Rana pipiens)

This frog is easy to identify, with its brown or green skin covered with large spots. The spots are rounded and have lightly colored borders. The northern leopard frog lives in marshes, moist fields, and mountain meadows. If you spot one, it will probably leap in a zigzag pattern to the safety of the nearest water. Its voice is low and sounds like a snore, followed by clucking noises. Listen for this noise at night in particular. This frog is found throughout the northern United States, except on the West Coast. The southern leopard frog has a longer pointed head, and only a few spots on its sides. It is active mainly at night, and its voice consists of throaty croaks.

Group: True frogs
Size: 2–3½ in (5–9 cm)
Distribution: The eastern and central regions of the U.S., including the South

Woodhouse's Toad

(Bufo woodhousii)
This toad has a light stripe on its back, obvious bony crests above its eyes, and dark spots with warty-looking bumps. Its general color is yellow to green to brown. It lives in many areas, including marshes, river bottoms, desert streams, backyards, and rain puddles. Woodhouse's toad becomes most active at night, and may be spotted catching insects that are attracted to light. It makes a sound rather like a bleating lamb.

Group: Toads
Size: 2½–5 in (6.5–12.5 cm)
Distribution: Common throughout most of the U.S.

Three-spine Stickleback
(Gasterosteus aculeatus)

This small fish gets its common name from the three sharp spines on its back. There are no scales on its body, just a row of bony plates along the sides. The top of its body is brownish-olive, while underneath it is white or silvery—males, however, have red bellies during the breeding season. The three-spine stickleback is not fussy about where it swims and lives in both salt and freshwater. It particularly likes shallow water where there are weeds growing. Look for stickleback nests in the spring. The males make them out of water plants and chase away other fish from their territory with their sharp spines. Three-spine sticklebacks feed on young shrimps, small fish, and fish eggs, as well as on plants.
Group: Sticklebacks
Size: Up to 2 in, on rare exceptions 4 in (5 cm, 10 cm)
Distribution: Pacific coast and Atlantic coast

Bluntnose Minnow
(Pimephales notatus)

You can see how this fish got its common name. Its snout is blunt, instead of pointed. The scales on its body are a silvery color, which are outlined in black and form a crisscross pattern. There is a strong black line running along each side. It has one short fin on its back. This minnow lives in several habitats, from small brooks to large lakes. It prefers water that is full of plant life, and it feeds on a variety of plants, as well as water insects and their larvae. Sometime between spring and fall, females lay their eggs under logs or stones.
Group: Carps and minnows
Size: Up to 3 in (7.5 cm)
Distribution: Eastern and central regions of Canada and the U.S.

White Sucker
(Catostomus commersoni)

This fish gets its common name from its suckerlike mouth, which has very obvious fleshy lips. Its body is olive-brown, with a silvery-white belly. It has a single short back fin. The white sucker lives in many different types of water, from fast-flowing to slow-moving, from weedy to clear. It creeps along the slimy bottom mud, feeding on insect larvae, mollusks, crustaceans, and algae. During the spring breeding season, the back of the male becomes lavender-colored and a red band appears along each side.

Group: Suckers
Size: Up to 18 in (45.5 cm)
Distribution: Southern Canada east of the Rockies and most of the central and eastern U.S.

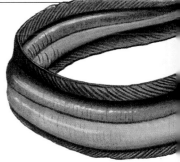

Spotted Flatworm
(Dugesia tigrina)

Like all flatworms, this creature has a thin, flat, soft body. As the name suggests, it has spots all over its body. The spotted flatworm has a triangular-shaped head and two simple, black eyespots. Its mouth is on the underside, and it crawls along the muddy bottoms of ponds, lakes, slow rivers, and streams, feeding on decaying matter. Flatworms look like blobs of jelly out of water. They will expand and glide around if put in a dish of water.
Group: Flatworms—Size: Up to ¾ in (2 cm)
Distribution: Common across North America

American Eel
(Anguilla rostrata)

All eels can be recognized by their snakelike shape, and the fins that run continuously along their long body. The American eel is sometimes called the silver eel because in its adult stage the skin color on its sides turns silver. This eel has a pointed snout and a wide mouth. It prefers muddy water but can be found in almost any type of water. Like other freshwater eels, the American eel undertakes a long journey after living in North American coastal waters for a few years. It migrates to the Sargasso Sea, an area of the Atlantic Ocean, where it spawns and then dies. The eggs hatch into larvae, which drift back to the North American coast. The larvae develop into young eels or "elvers." The females enter the freshwater streams and rivers; the males are believed to remain in salt waters. The eels mature and then the cycle starts all over again.
Group: Eels—Size: 1½–4 ft (0.5–1.25 m) depending on sex
Distribution: Atlantic and Gulf coasts and coastal rivers of North America

Flatworm
(Order: Tricladida)

There are many different kinds of flatworms and most are difficult to identify. This flatworm is blackish in color and has a pointed head. It lives in springs and headwaters, creeping along the bottom and feeding on small living invertebrates or on dead and decaying matter.
Group: Flatworms
Size: Up to ¾ in (2 cm)
Distribution: Common across the U.S.

Sludge Worms
(Tubifex tubifex)

Sludge, or mud worms, are long, thin, and reddish in color. These worms live in the mud at the bottom of lakes, stagnant ponds, or polluted rivers. They are able to survive in poor conditions. They build soft mud tubes in which they live head down, with their tails waving about in the water. You may see them in aquarium shops, where they are sold as food for fish.
Group: Tubifex worms—Size: Up to 2 in (5 cm)
Distribution: Widespread throughout North America

Mollusks

Spire Snail
(Amnicola)

These tiny snails have a shell with four to five whorls (one complete rotation of a shell's spiral is a whorl). Spire snails' shells may be reddish-brown, grayish-brown, or tan in color. They live in many kinds of freshwater habitats among thick weeds and prefer unpolluted water. As with many snails, the spire snail can survive out of water for a time by closing the opening of its shell with a plate called an "operculum."
Group: Spire shells
Size: Up to ¼ in (0.5 cm)
Distribution: Widespread throughout North America

Flat-ended Spire Snail
(Amnicola)

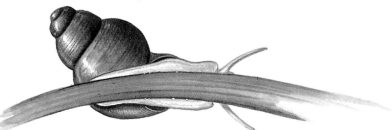

This type of spire snail is quite wide and solid. Its shell has about five complete turns, or "whorls," but the first two whorls are sunken below the third, which is the largest. The "spire" at the top is barrel-shaped. This snail lives in lakes, ponds, and rivers of any size, and it tends to stay near plant life or on sandy or muddy bottoms. Its body is white.
Group: Spire shells—Size: Up to ¼ in (0.5 cm)
Distribution: Most of Canada and the eastern and central regions of the U.S.

Pea Clam
(Pisidium spp.*)*

Also called pea-shell cockles, these little creatures have shells in two parts, so they are bivalves. The shells are yellowish or buff in color and rounded in shape. They can be found in many watery habitats, even in drinking troughs for livestock animals. They sometimes burrow into gravel or sand on the bottom of the water. Left in a bowl of water, pea clams may send out two short, joined siphon tubes, through which   they draw in water.

Group: Orb mussels
Size: Up to ¼ in (0.5 cm)
Distribution: Found throughout North America

Fingernail Clam
(Sphaerium spp.*)*

Also called orb-shell cockles, these bivalves are yellowish- or grayish-brown and rounded. They are slightly bigger than pea clams. Fingernail clams burrow into the bottom of various freshwater habitats. Young ones may move about on water plants. If you collect some specimens and put them into water, you may see a clam extend its two siphon tubes and strong foot outside of its shell.

Group:
Orb mussels
Size: Up to ½ in (1 cm)
Distribution: Throughout
North America

Eastern Lampmussel
(Lampsilis radiata radiata)

This mussel has a wide, dark brown to black shell covered with wide markings. It gets the name "lampmussel" because the markings look like rays of light. The lampmussel is common in rivers and lakes of all sizes, where it lives on gravel, sand, or mud bottoms, filtering plankton from the water.
Group: Pearly mussels
Size: Up to 4 in (10 cm)
Distribution: Lower St. Lawrence Seaway system, south to South Carolina River system

Fatmucket
(Lampsilis siliquoidea)

The fatmucket is similar in form to the lampmussel, but its shell is yellowish, greenish, or brownish, and the raylike markings are narrow instead of wide. This bivalve lives in rivers and lakes of all sizes. The young attach themselves to various types of fish, including white bass, white crappie, and yellow perch. They feed off the fish a few weeks, then drop off to live at the lake or river bottom.
Group: Pearly mussels
Size: Up to 5 in (12.5 cm) long
Distribution: Canada and the eastern and central U.S.

Eastern Elliptio
(Elliptio complanata)

This mussel has a shell in two parts, so it is a bivalve. Each shell is oval in shape. The shell's outside is rough in texture and brown or black in color. Inside, it has a pearly coating. The elliptio lives on the bottom of shallow ponds, rivers, lakes, and streams. Like all mussels, the elliptio sucks in water through a tube, or siphon. It then filters out food, usually plankton, and ejects the waste water through a second siphon. An elliptio attaches itself to the side of a fish and feeds off the fish for the first few weeks of life.

Group: Pearly mussels—Size: 3–4 in (7.5–10 cm)
Distribution: Southeastern Canada and the eastern coast of the U.S.

A Collecting Trip

You don't need much equipment, and you certainly don't need to be an expert naturalist to find and study water creatures. Wear old clothes and waterproof footgear, as the area around a pond may be quite muddy. Don't forget to take this field guide! When you get there, don't run, stamp around on the bank, or shout. The noise will frighten animals away.

What to take

You may also find the following things useful:
1 **Underwater viewing box** (see the description at right for how to make it).
2 **Empty, white margarine or ice cream container** for collecting and watching your catch.
3 **An eyedropper or paintbrush** for moving small animals without hurting them.
4 **Glass or plastic jars with screw-on lids** for carrying specimens home.
5 **Your field notebook, with pens and pencils** for notetaking.
6 **A magnifying glass**. Buy one labeled X 4 or X 6 and wear it on a string around your neck.
7 **A camera** to record the various sites.
8 **Moist towelettes** to clean your hands after handling animals.
9 **A lightweight backpack** to carry everything in.

See the advice on handling amphibians on the next page before you begin collecting.

SAFETY DOs and DON'Ts

1 **Always tell an adult** where you are going before any expedition to a pond or river.
2 **Always take a friend**.
3 **Always test the depth of water with a long stick or branch** before going wading—the water may be deeper than you think!
4 **Always test any log or stone** before you use it as a stepping stone.
5 **Always wear a life jacket** if you are going out in a boat—even if you can swim well.
6 **Don't lean too far over the water's edge.**
7 **Don't climb on tree branches overhanging** the water—they might break.

Underwater viewing box

Make your own viewing box so that you can watch water creatures in their natural habitat.
1 **Find a plastic container,** such as an old bucket or wastepaper basket. Get an adult to cut the bottom out of the container, leaving a rim about an inch (2.5 centimeters) wide.

Handling amphibians

Should you catch a frog, toad, salamander, or newt, be very careful how you handle it. Some of these animals could be endangered, and to harm one would be bad for the environment. Further, some animals might live in ponds with water that is contaminated. Wash your hands after handling amphibians to remove the bacteria that may be on your skin. Always ask a responsible adult before setting out to catch amphibians, because some toads and a few salamanders can secrete an unpleasant liquid from their skins. This liquid can cause swelling and discomfort if it enters a cut. **Rinse the affected part with clean water as soon as possible if this happens. Be careful not to rub your eyes or put your hand to your mouth after touching amphibians. Their chemical secretions can also cause your mouth or eyelids to swell and burn.**

Keeping records

Making notes and quick drawings in your field notebook will help you identify fast-moving animals. Transfer your notes into a ring binder or a computer program when you get home and record each trip on a separate sheet of paper or as a separate database entry. File your sketches, photos, and any other samples you may have collected during your expedition.

1 **When you visit a new site,** give it a name, write down the date, and note what sort of habitat it is (pond, river, marsh, etc.).
2 **Each time you visit that site,** record what the weather was like and what time of day it was.
3 **When you see an animal,** watch it carefully. Make a note of its shape, color, and size to help identification.
4 **Write down what the animal was doing** (swimming, eating, resting, etc.), and if it was making a noise. Also, note how many animals of that kind you saw during your visit.

2 **Get an adult to cut a piece of sturdy clear plastic** to fit inside the container.
3 **Stick it down on to the rim** with waterproof adhesive—you can buy this from a pet store.
4 **Take your viewing box along to a shallow pond,** lake, or reservoir. Carefully lean over the bank and place the clear plastic end of your box in the water. Look through the hole to see crawling snails, swimming fish, and other active creatures.
5 **You can also wade upstream** in shallow streams and rivers, wearing your rubber boots. These areas are good for finding mussels. A sunny day is best.

Ponds & Shallow Lakes

Ponds have still, shallow water. Shallow water lets light penetrate to the bottom, allowing water weeds to grow there. These weeds provide food and shelter for many animals. Because the water is still, there is not very much oxygen in it, and it may be stagnant (foul and slimy) near the bottom.

Many pond snails, and all frogs, toads, newts, and reptiles can live in stagnant water, because they come to the surface to breathe. Other pond animals, such as mudpuppies and tadpoles, have very large gills to help them take enough oxygen from the water.

Small ponds often have to be looked after to stop sedges, rushes, and other swamp plants from growing right into them and filling them. Any animals found in ponds and lakes will also be found in slow-moving rivers (see pages 72–77), where conditions are very similar to a pond.

As many natural wetlands are now being destroyed, ponds are becoming a more important refuge for water animals. This picture shows several from this book—see how many you can identify.

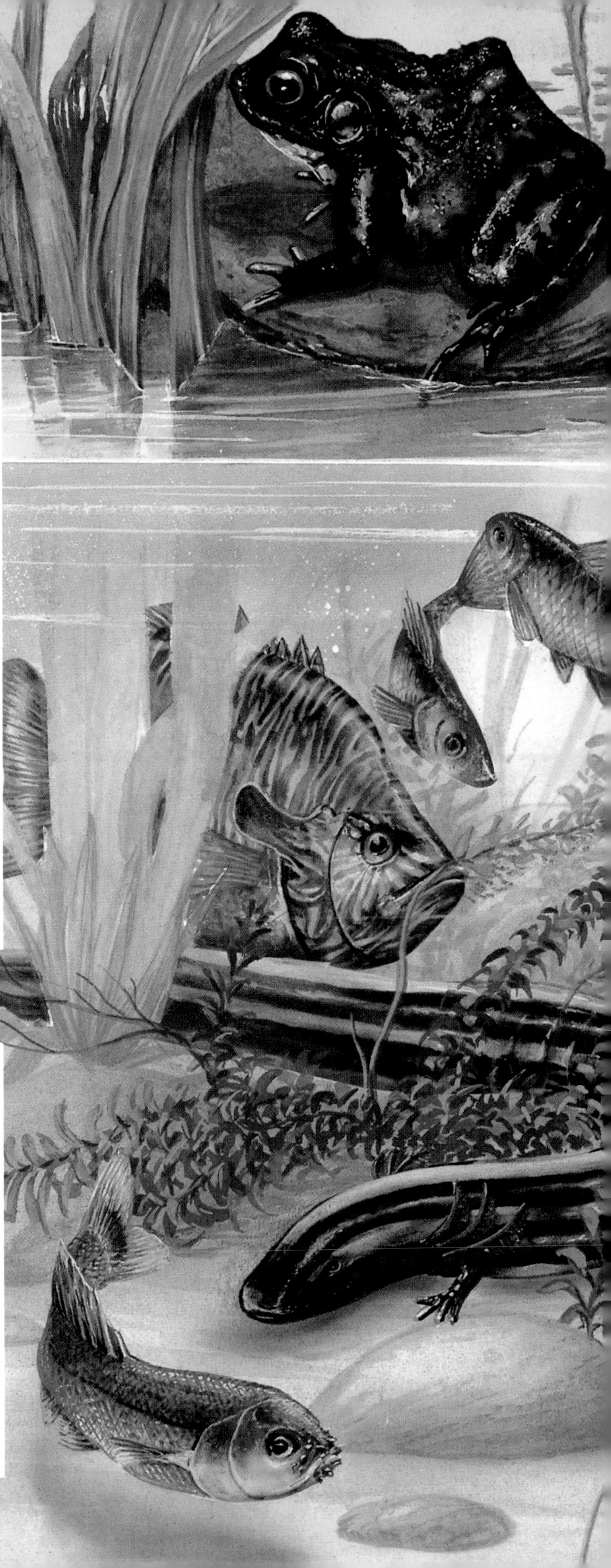

Reptiles

Chicken Turtle
(Deirochelys reticularia)

You will recognize this turtle by its long, stripy neck—it is nearly as long as its shell. The shell itself is green or brown, with a yellowish, netlike pattern and an orange or yellow border. The chicken turtle lives in plant-filled ponds and lakes, ditches, or swamps. It feeds on small water creatures such as tadpoles. You may see it basking in the sun, or sometimes crossing highways.
Group: Pond and box turtles—Size: 4–10 in (10–25 cm)
Distribution: Southeastern and south-central U.S.

Western Pond Turtle
(Clemmys marmorata)

This turtle has a smooth, somewhat flat, olive-brown shell with dark flecks. It lives in weedy ponds, marshes, rivers, streams, and ditches, where it feeds on plants, insects, worms, and fish. It likes to sunbathe out of the water, but it will dive back in if you disturb it.
Group: Pond and box turtles—Size: 3–7 in (7.5–17.5 cm)
Distribution: West coast of North America from British Columbia in Canada to Baja California in Mexico

Spotted Turtle
(Clemmys guttata)

This small turtle is easy to recognize with its smooth, black shell dotted with yellow spots. There are also spots on its head, neck, and legs. The undershell is creamy-yellow with black blotches around the edge. Females have orange eyes, while males have brown eyes. Look for them in marshy meadows and boglands, as well as in ponds and shallow, muddy-bottomed streams. This turtle likes to sunbathe in the spring, often on a log at the water's edge. Favorite foods include insects and water plants.
Group: Pond and box turtles—Size: 3½–5 in (9–12.5 cm)
Distribution: Coastal plain of the eastern U.S. and the southern area bordering the Great Lakes

Pond Slider
(Trachemys scripta)

The name for one type of pond slider, the yellow-bellied slider, comes from the yellowish blotches on the lower shell. It also has yellow blotches behind its eyes, as shown here. The turtle's shell is oval in shape, olive-brown in color, and patterned with yellow marks. It lives in slow rivers, shallow streams, swamps, and ponds with lots of plant life and soft bottoms. Young sliders feed on water insects, mollusks, and crustaceans. When older, the turtle becomes a plant-eater.
**Group: Pond and box turtles
Size: 5–12 in (12.5–30 cm)
Distribution: Southeastern and southern U.S., south to Brazil**

Florida Softshell
(Apalone ferox)

The Florida softshell, as its name would suggest, has no hard shell; its shell looks something like a brownish-gray, leathery pancake! It also has an unusual tubelike snout and a long neck. Its soft shell is thickened all around the edge and has small bumps at the front. Look for this turtle swimming in sandy-bottomed lakes, ponds, and canals, with just its snout visible. It also likes to bask in the sun, sitting on banks or logs. It feeds on crayfish, snails, frogs, and fish. **Be careful if you handle a softshell, as it has surprisingly sharp teeth.**
Group: Softshell turtles—Size: 6–12 in (15–30 cm)
Distribution: Southeastern U.S.

Mud Snake
(Farancia abacura)

This big, black, shiny snake has triangular pink or red bars on its sides and a red belly. Smooth scales cover the body, and there is a sharp spine at the end of its tail; this spine is not poisonous. The mud snake lives around swampy lakes and slow-flowing, muddy-bottomed streams. On rainy nights you may see it crossing roads in swampy areas. It feeds mostly on amphiumas and "sirens" (see page 27).
Group: Colubrid snakes—Size: 3–6½ ft (0.9–2 m)
Distribution: Southeastern, western, and south-midwestern regions of the U.S.

Eastern Ribbon Snake
(Thamnophis sauritus)

A slim, stripy snake, the eastern ribbon snake is olive-brown where it is not striped. The stripes are thin and are usually orange-tan and cream. This snake lives around weedy lakes and in marshes, ditches, streams, and rivers. If frightened, it slithers into the water and glides away across the surface. It feeds at the water's edge on frogs, salamanders, and small fish. Female eastern ribbon snakes give birth to live young.
Group: Colubrid snakes
Size: 1½–4 ft
(0.5–1.2 m)
Distribution:
Eastern half
of the U.S.

Southern Water Snake
(Nerodia fasciata)

This snake has a stout body, which usually has dark bands running across it. However, it may have only light stripes on its back, or no pattern at all. There are large blotches or wormlike marks on the belly. It lives in lakes, ponds, swamps, marshes, and slow-moving streams. It becomes active at night, when it feeds on frogs, tadpoles, and fish. Females give birth to live young.
Group: Colubrid snakes—Size: 1½–5 ft (0.5–1.5 m)
Distribution: Southern, western, and south-midwestern regions of the U.S.

Amphibians

Ponds & Shallow Lakes

Bullfrog
(Rana catesbeiana)

This frog is hard to miss. It is the biggest frog in North America and is colored green or yellow with dark gray mottling on its back. Its belly is cream—often also with mottled gray markings. The round eardrum behind the eye is very large. The bullfrog lives in lakes, ponds, bogs, and slow-flowing streams. It can often be seen sitting at the water's edge, but it will quickly flee if anyone comes along. Favorite foods include insects, crayfish, other frogs, and minnows. It is most active at night. Listen for the bullfrog's loud voice. It sounds as if it is saying "jug o' rum."

Group: True frogs
Size: 3–8 in (7.5–20.5 cm)
Distribution: Eastern and central U.S., eastern Canada, introduced in the west

Red-legged Frog
(Rana aurora)

This frog gets its name from the red color on the underside of its hind legs. Its back is reddish-brown to gray, with darker specks and blotches, and its belly is yellow fading into red. It usually also has a dark patch over and behind the eye with a white jaw stripe. The red-legged frog lives near ponds and lakes that are full of plants. It also likes damp forests and woodlands. It is most active during the day, and its voice consists of a series of throaty notes.

Group: True frogs
Size: 2–6 in (5–15 cm)
Distribution: Western coast of North America from Vancouver Island to the peninsula of Baja California in Mexico

Spring Peeper
(Pseudacris crucifer)

The little spring peeper can be tan, brown, or gray, with a dark cross on its back. It lives in woodland areas, near ponds or swamps and becomes most active at night. The peeper makes a high-pitched whistle that sounds like the jingling of bells when a group of them sing together. This sound is one of the first signals that spring has arrived. The groups often form in trees or shrubs.

Group: Tree frogs—Size: ¾–1½ in (2–3.5 cm)
Distribution: Most of southeast Canada and the eastern half of the U.S.

Northern Cricket Frog
(Acris crepitans)

Group: Tree frogs
Size: ¾–1½ in (2–3.5 cm)
Distribution: Most of the eastern U.S., except the Florida panhandle

This knobby skinned frog is colored greenish-brown, yellow, red, or black. It has a dark triangle between its eyes and a dark stripe on its outer thigh. Its legs are quite short. This frog lives in ponds with shallow water and a lot of plants, or by slow-flowing streams. It is active during the day, and there are often many of them around, but you probably won't catch one because they move too quickly. The northern cricket frog's voice sounds like a series of clicks, similar to a cricket's song.

Green Frog
(Rana clamitans)

Although it is called a green frog, this frog can be brown or bronze in color as well. Two raised ridges run down both sides of the back. Its belly is white, with a pattern of lines or spots. Males can be identified by their yellow throat. The green frog can be seen in shallow fresh water, such as springs, swamps, brooks, or the banks of ponds and lakes. It usually becomes active at night and makes a noise like the twang of a loose banjo string.

Group: True frogs
Size: 2–4 in (5–10 cm)
Distribution: Common throughout eastern North America

Many-lined Salamander
(Stereochilus marginatus)

This salamander is so called because of the many dark lines along its sides. Its overall color is brown or dull yellow, and it has a yellow belly with speckles. It also has a small head and a short tail. Look for this salamander in ponds, slow streams, and swampy areas. It is usually in the water, but it sometimes sits under logs where the ground is damp.

Group: Lungless salamanders
Size: 2–5 in (5–12.5 cm)
Distribution: Much of the East Coast of the U.S.

Amphibians

Ponds & Shallow Lakes

Red-spotted Newt

(Notophthalmus viridescens viridescens)
This newt is yellowish-brown or olive-green with black-bordered red spots on its back. At a younger stage—a newt in this stage is called an eft—it is bright orange-red in color. The adult newt lives in ponds, small lakes, marshes, streams, and in the damp woodlands nearby these bodies of water. It feeds on worms, insects, crustaceans, and mollusks. The efts are very bold and may be seen on the forest floor after a summer shower.
Group: Newts—Size: 4 in (10 cm)
Distribution: Southeastern Canada and eastern, southern, and midwestern regions of the U.S.

Broken-striped Newt

(Notophthalmus viridescens dorsalis)

The broken-striped newt is so called because of the broken black-bordered red stripe that runs down its back. It is yellowish-brown or olive-green in color. The young, land-dwelling eft, shown here, is reddish-brown and has red stripes with a less-defined border than is seen on the adult. The adult newt lives in pools, ponds, ditches, and the quiet parts of streams. The efts can be found under logs in damp places.
Group: Newts—Size: 2¾–5½ in (7–14 cm)
Distribution: North Carolina and South Carolina—other varieties can be found throughout the eastern U.S.

California Newt

(Taricha torosa)

This newt has rough skin, which is tan to reddish-brown on the back, and yellow to orange on the belly. The eyes are large with light-colored lower lids. In the mating season, males become smooth-skinned. The California newt lives in quiet streams, ponds, or lakes, and in the surrounding evergreen and oak forests. During a rainy season you may see this newt by day, but when it is dry, it burrows under moist leaf litter. When threatened, it reveals its brightly colored belly to frighten off predators.
Group: Newts
Size: 5–8 in (12.5–20 cm)
Distribution: Coastal California

Rough-skinned Newt

(Taricha granulosa)

It is difficult to tell this newt from the California newt. This newt, however, has even rougher bumpy skin, and it is light brown to black on the back, and bright yellow or orange on the belly. Its eyes are small, with dark lower lids. In the mating season, males develop smooth skin. The rough-skinned newt lives in ponds, lakes, and streams that have plant life, or in surrounding moist woodlands. It is very fond of the water, but you may see it on land on humid days. If threatened, it assumes a warning pose to frighten off its attacker.
Group: Newts
Size: 5–8½ in (12.5–21.5 cm)
Distribution: Pacific coast of the U.S. and Canada

Dwarf Siren

(Pseudobranchus striatus)

Sirens are a type of salamander. Unlike most salamanders, however, sirens never get past the larval stage, meaning they do not develop adult characteristics. You can see the gills close to the head. Called the dwarf siren because it is the smallest siren of all, this creature lives in ditches, swamps, and weedy ponds. It is brown or light gray with light stripes on its sides.

Group: Sirens
Size: 4–9 in (10–23 cm)
Distribution: South Carolina, Georgia, and Florida in the U.S.

Siren

(Family: Sirenidae)

Sirens are salamanders that live in quiet, weedy waters. With their long, slender bodies, they look much like eels. They have visible gills at the neck, no hind legs, and tiny front legs. They feed at night, mainly on small animals. If the water in their home dries up, they burrow into the mud and survive by covering themselves with a sticky cocoon, which keeps in the moisture.

Group: Sirens
Size: 7–36 in (18–90 cm)
Distribution: Coastal areas of the southeastern U.S.

Amphiuma

(Family: Amphiumidae)

Amphiumas are another type of salamander. They have long, slender bodies and, like sirens, they also look like eels. They have four tiny legs that are no longer used by the animal—each leg has one to three toes depending on the species. Amphiumas do not change much from the larva form. They lose their gills, but the gill slits can still be seen. They are active at night and feed on creatures such as crayfish, frogs, snakes, fish, and even other amphiumas. They can be seen in muddy ditches, ponds, swamps, and streams. **Be careful if you find an amphiuma, because they give a nasty bite!**
Group: Amphiumas
Size: Up to 45 in (110 cm)
Distribution: Coastal areas of the southeastern U.S.

Red Shiner
(Cyprinella lutrensis)

This fish is a brilliant steel-blue color with large, diamond-shaped scales. It has an arched back and red fins, except for the back fin. The red shiner lives in ponds, slow-flowing streams, and large rivers that flow over sand or gravel. It feeds on bits of water plants, small insects, and crustaceans. In the early summer, females lay their eggs on plants under the water. Another name for this fish is the African fire barb. It is often called by this name when sold as an aquarium fish.
Group: Carps and minnows
Size: Up to 3 in (7.5 cm)
Distribution: Central U.S.

Goldfish
(Carassius auratus)

You've probably seen this fish more often in fish bowls than in the wild, but it has been introduced into warmer waters in North America. As its name suggests, the goldfish often is a goldish-orange color. Goldfish living in the wild tend to be plain-colored, however. It has a long back fin that has one serrated spine. This fish likes warm water that has plenty of plants in it, where it feeds on these plants, and on water insects, mollusks, and crustaceans.
Group: Carps and minnows
Size: 2–12 in (5–30 cm)
Distribution: Warmer waters of the U.S., Canada, and Mexico

Channel Catfish
(Ictalurus punctatus)

This catfish can be recognized by its spotty body and forked tail. It is a slate-brown color above and silvery-white below. Long barbels surround its mouth and, like all catfish, its skin is smooth and has no scales. The channel catfish lives in ponds, lakes, reservoirs, or large rivers that flow over gravel or sand. It feeds on other fish, insects, mollusks, and crayfish, mainly at night. Females lay their eggs under a stone or in a nest below the bank of a stream, and the males guard the nest.
Group: Catfishes—Size: Up to 48 in (120 cm)
Distribution: Found across the eastern region of the U.S. and into Mexico

Common Carp
(Cyprinus carpio)

This carp can be recognized by its fat body, scales that have a crisscross pattern, and a long back fin. At the top of this fin is a hard, serrated ray, but the rest of the rays are soft. The carp is a golden-olive color and has two short barbels on each side of its jaw. It prefers to live in warm water and can be seen in quiet ponds, lakes, and sluggish rivers with plants in them. Favorite foods include mollusks, crustaceans, and insect larvae, as well as algae and plants. In the spring, female carp lay their eggs; these eggs may stick to surrounding plants or sink in the water to the bottom.
Group: Carps and minnows
Size: Up to 40 in (76 cm)
Distribution: Southern Canada and throughout the U.S.

Golden Shiner
(Notemigonus crysoleucas)

The young of this deep-bodied minnow start off silvery in color, becoming golden as they get older. This fish prefers to swim in quiet, weedy ponds, swamps, and streams, where it feeds on plankton, water insects, mollusks, and algae. These fish tend to swim in a group. Females lay their eggs in midsummer. These eggs stick to underwater plants.
Group: Carps and minnows
Size: Up to 12 in (30 cm)
Distribution: Native to southern Canada and eastern North America, but introduced elsewhere

Nine-spine Stickleback
(Pungitius pungitius)

This fish is slender, and, as its name suggests, has a row of spines on its back. It can actually have between 7 and 12 of them. Its color is dull brown and blotchy above and silvery on its belly. It may live in fresh or salt water, as long as the water is cold. It prefers densely weeded small ponds and streams.
Group: Sticklebacks
Size: Up to 2 in (5 cm)
Distribution: Cold northern waters in North America

Northern Pike
(Esox lucius)

This big fish is easy to recognize, with its long body and duckbill-shaped snout. Its jaws are lined with sharp, pointed teeth. The pike eats fish, frogs, insects, mice, and even birds. The pike's body is greenish, with white or yellow spots. It swims in cold-water lakes, reservoirs, and weed-choked rivers. It can live for more than 20 years.
Group: Pikes—Size: Up to 48 in (120 cm)
Distribution: Alaska, Canada, and northern areas of the eastern and central continental U.S.

Brown Bullhead
(Ictalurus nebulosus)

This is a type of catfish, and it has dark growths called barbels on its chin. It is yellowish-brown, olive, or bluish-black with a yellowish or milk-white belly. As with all catfish, there is a small, rayless fin between its back and tail fins. The brown bullhead lives in muddy-bottomed ponds and lakes, and slow streams and rivers. It uses its barbels to feel along the bottom muck for the insect larvae and mollusks that it eats. The female scoops a hollow in the mud, where she lays her eggs. The male then guards the eggs.
Group: Catfishes—Size: Up to 21 in (53 cm)
Distribution: Southern Canada and the eastern U.S.

Fish

Northern Red-belly Dace
(Phoxinus eos)

This small fish is so named because the male has a red belly in the breeding season. This dace has dark stripes along its greenish-brown back—the belly is normally white. The scales are so small that the fish appears to have none. Its fins may have a yellow tinge, and its tail fin is forked. It is common around the swampy edges of ponds and lakes. It also lives in brooks, springs, and small streams that have gravel on the bottom. It feeds mainly on algae but will also eat water insects.
Group: Carps and minnows
Size: Up to 2½ in (6.5 cm)
Distribution: Eastern U.S.

Longear Sunfish
(Lepomis megalotis)

This brightly colored sunfish gets its name from its very long gill flap, which looks something like an ear. It has blue-green, wavy lines on its stout body, and its belly is orange. Its back fin has spines, which give it a jagged appearance. Look for this fish in lakes, reservoirs, and small, clear streams and rivers that have gravel and rock on the bottom. It feeds on water insects, crustaceans, and small fish. Males dig a nest in the gravel in the summer, the females then lay their eggs into such nests.
Group: Sunfishes—Size: Up to 7 in (18 cm)
Distribution: Southeastern Canada and the eastern U.S.

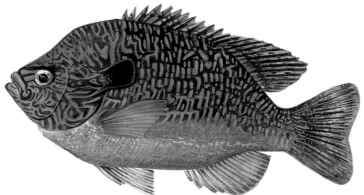

Fathead Minnow
(Pimephales promelas)

This unusual-looking fish has a fat body and a head that looks flattened on top. Its back fin is round and starts with a blunt-tipped half-ray. This minnow has a dark olive back, with yellowish sides, and a white or cream belly. It lives in small streams, ditches, and boggy lakes with soft mud bottoms. In the mating season, the male's color darkens and he develops little knobs on his head, as shown. Fathead minnows feed on algae and plankton.
Group: Carps and minnows
Size: Up to 3 in (7.5 cm)
Distribution: Throughout central North America

Pumpkinseed
(Lepomis gibbosus)

This fish is also called the common sunfish. It has a thick body, which is tan or pale yellow, and its sides are covered in spots. There is also a scattering of tiny brown spots on the tail fin. A good identification guide is the black and orange tip of the ear flap. The back fin has stiff spines. You'll find the pumpkinseed swimming in streams, ponds, and lakes with plenty of plants in them. It feeds on mollusks, insects, and fish. In the summer, males scoop out saucer-shaped nests in the bottom sand or gravel. Then females lay their eggs into these nests.
Group: Sunfishes—Size: Up to 8 in (20 cm)
Distribution: Canada and the Atlantic coast, the Great Lakes, and the upper Mississippi River Valley

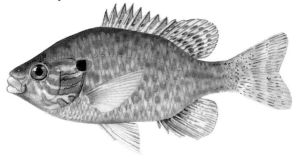

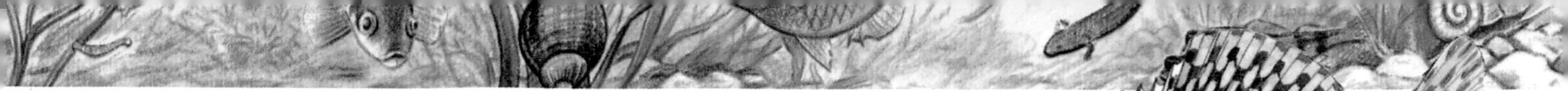

(Pomoxis annularis)

This fish is silvery-olive in color with several dark markings running down each side of its body. The fins are very mottled in appearance; the back fin has spines. The white crappie lives in streams, rivers, ponds, lakes, and reservoirs, where it feeds on water insects and plankton as a young fish. When it grows bigger, its diet changes to include fish, mollusks, and crustaceans. The male white crappie builds a nest, which it then guards, a habit that earned it its other common name of bachelor perch. Many people like the taste of this fish, so it is very popular with anglers.

White Crappie

Group: Sunfishes—Size: Up to 15 in (38 cm)
Distribution: Southern Ontario in Canada and much of the U.S., except the west

Bluegill
(Lepomis macrochirus)

This fish may be blue, as shown here, but it can also be yellow or brown. There are several vertical bars on its sides. In the breeding season, males become bright orange on their bellies. The bluegill has a small mouth and feeds on mollusks, worms, and water insects. It prefers to live in warm-water habitats in weedy ponds, lakes, streams, and rivers. Males dig out shallow nests from the bottom sand during the summer. Bluegills are a favorite with fishermen.

Group: Sunfishes—Size: Up to 10 in (25.5 cm)
Distribution: Southeastern Canada and most of the U.S., except the west

Largemouth Bass
(Micropterus salmoides)

This fish gets its common name from its big mouth, which stretches back farther on each side of its face than its eye. Its lower lip sticks out beyond the upper one. The largemouth bass is quite streamlined in shape and is green with brown mottling. Its back fin has stiff spines. It lives in shallow, weedy, lakes, or in ponds or reservoirs, where it feeds mainly on insects, crayfish, frogs, and fish. The male builds a nest in the spring. When the young hatch, they swim around in a group or "school," sometimes for as long as a month. The largemouth bass is one of the most popular game fish in the United States and is much sought by anglers.

Group: Sunfishes—Size: 18 in (45.5 cm)
Distribution: Southern Ontario, in Canada and most of the U.S., except the west

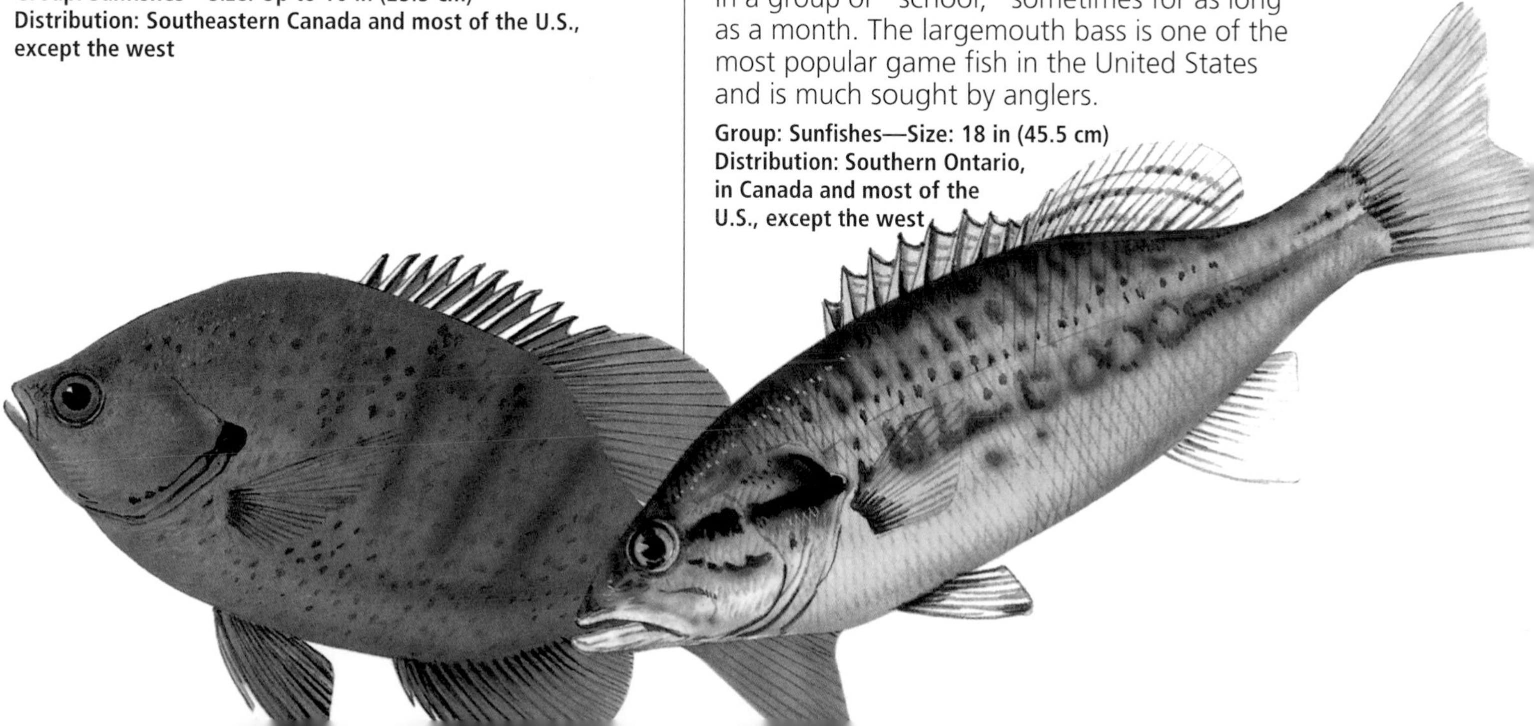

Explore a Pond

Check with your teacher or an expert at a nature center before doing these activities. That adult may recommend a different activity more appropriate for your locality. Nature activities can be harmful to animals or their environment, or to you, so it always is best to get expert advice and to have an adult along on any expedition.

Pond dipping

Pond dipping is exactly what it sounds like: it involves dipping a net into a pond and seeing what you catch. Spring is probably the best time to go pond dipping. There are not as many weeds then, and there are a lot of adult beetles, bugs, tadpoles, and newts.

1 **You will need a simple net with a mesh of about 2 millimeters**. If the mesh is too fine it will clog up. If it is too big, it won't catch anything small.
2 **Quietly approach the water's edge.** Any sudden noise or movement will send the pond animals into hiding.
3 **Sweep your net across the surface of the pond** for surface-dwelling insects like beetles, pond skaters, water boatmen, and water mites.
4 **Scoop the net gently under pond weeds,** brushing the weed to knock off animals living and crawling on it, such as tadpoles, damsel fly nymphs, May fly nymphs, or snails.
5 **Gently push the net along the surface of the bottom mud**. (Be careful not to scoop too deep or your net will fill up with muck.) Here, you may find flatworms, caddisfly cases, worms, and shrimps.
6 **Put your finds into some containers,** along with water from the pond.
7 **When you have finished examining your specimens**, gently return them to the water.

Be careful which animals you put together: newts, beetle larvae, and dragonfly nymphs will eat other animals such as tadpoles. If you handle the animals without wearing gloves, be sure to wash your hands right away.

Examining very small animals

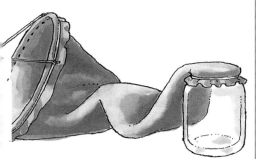

1 **Make a tapering net with a very fine mesh.** Cut one leg off of a pair of panty hose. Then take an embroidery hoop and attach 4 lengths of string at equal points around the circumference of the inner ring of the hoop. Place the stocking through the outer ring. Stretch the top of the stocking around and over the ring. Snap the inner ring inside the outer ring. Tie the strings as shown.

2 **Cut a hole in foot end of the stocking** and tie the end around the mouth of a jelly jar.

3 **Walk around the pond trailing the net with its jar** in clear water above the bottom and away from weeds. The animals you catch will be washed down into the jar.

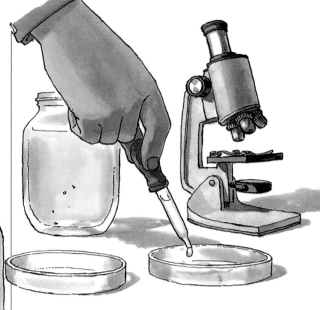

4 **Lift the jar up and look at it.** It should be full of tiny animals, such as water fleas and copepods. Use your magnifying glass to examine your catch.

5 **If you have a microscope,** you can use it to look at your catch more closely. Use an eyedropper to transfer drops of collected pond water to a slide.

Mud grubbing

The mud at the bottom of a pond is a good place to look for worms and other animals that can put up with low oxygen levels and not much light. The best way to find these is to scoop up some mud and debris with your net or bucket and sieve it, a little at a time (use an old kitchen sieve). Hold the sieve halfway submerged in the water, and shake it gently so that the mud floats away, leaving the animals behind.

Mollusks

Ponds & Shallow Lakes

Gyralus

This snail has a shell with four rounded whorls (each whorl is one turn of a spiral shell). The shell is glossy and light to dark brown in color. This snail is common and lives in many types of freshwater habitats, especially those with muddy bottoms. It lives on submerged water plants.
Group: Ramshorn snails
Size: Up to ¼ in (0.5 cm)
Distribution: Found throughout Canada and the U.S.

Common Tadpole Snail

(Physa heterostropha)

This snail is also called the bladder snail because its shell is like a sac or a bladder. The shell has a large opening on the left side but only a tiny spire. It is yellow or brown in color. The tadpole snail lives in rivers, streams, ponds, and stagnant pools, and feeds mainly on plants. It needs to come to the water's surface to breathe.
Group: Bladder snails
Size: ½–1 in (1–2.5 cm)
Distribution: Found throughout Canada and the U.S.

American Ear Snail

(Pseudosuccinea collumella)

This snail's shell has a huge aperture (opening) in proportion to the size of its shell. The shell is spiral in shape, with a short, narrow cone at the top, and it is light greenish-brown to yellowish-brown. The last whorl before the opening has an earlike flare, which gives the snail its name. You'll find the ear snail in lakes, ponds, and slow-flowing streams among lily pads and reeds.
Group: Pond snails
Size: Up to 1 in (2.5 cm)
Distribution: Found throughout the eastern U.S.; introduced in the western U.S.

Three-whorled Ramshorn

(Nelisoma trivolvis)

Can you see how this small snail got its common name? Its shell looks like a ram's horn and has three distinct whorls. Other species of ramshorn may have four or five whorls, but in all of them the shell is flat and coiled with no spire. Most are brown or chestnut colored. The ramshorn can be found in lakes, ponds, and slow streams, where there is plenty of plant life to feed on. It breathes air, so it must regularly come to the water's surface to survive.
Group: Ramshorn snails
Size: ½–1¼ in (1–3 cm)
Distribution: Eastern U.S. diagonally north to western Canada

Great Pond Snail
(Lymnaea stagnalis)

This snail has a tan-colored, almost transparent shell, with a sharp spire on the top. The first whorl is large, up to half the total height. It is also called the stagnant pond snail because it can survive in stagnant waters (still, foul waters with low levels of oxygen). It can survive such water because it comes to the surface at regular intervals to breathe and does not use gills. It can be found in large ponds and lakes, as well as in ditches and marshes.
Group: Pond snails
Size: 1½–2 in (4–5 cm)
Distribution: Found throughout most of Canada and the U.S.

Florida Apple Snail
(Pomacea paludosa)

This large snail has a rounded, smooth shell that is olive-brown in color with brown bands encircling it. It lives in still lakes and slow-flowing rivers and uses gills to extract oxygen from the water. It feeds on plants. Females lay a huge mass of eggs on plant stems above the water. The young snails hatch and then drop into the water.
Group: Apple snails
Size: 2–2½ in (5–6 cm)
Distribution: Florida

Georgian Mystery Snail
(Viviparus georgianus)

This large snail has a glossy, olive-green shell with a round opening and a high spire. The whorls are rounded, and usually have brown bands. It gives birth to live young instead of laying eggs. The mystery snail lives in ponds, lakes, and slow rivers, where it feeds on algae.
Group: River snails
Size: 1½–2 in (4–5 cm)
Distribution: Eastern U.S. and southeastern Canada

Valve Snail
(Valvata spp.)

The valve snail lives in large lakes, usually on the mud among plant life. There are many species of valve snails in North America. Their shell is sometimes white, but it may also be pale brown or brown in color. When the valve snail retreats into its shell, it seals the opening with a round, horny plate called the operculum.
Group: Valve snails
Size: Up to ¼ in (0.5 cm)
Distribution: Canada and the northeastern U.S.

Crustaceans

Ponds & Shallow Lakes

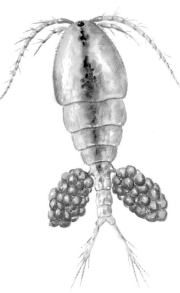

Copepod
(Subclass: Copepoda)

There are thousands of species (types) of these tiny creatures. Some species live in any kind of still, freshwater habitat, from ponds to puddles. They use their legs or their antennae to propel themselves as they swim. Females have egg sacs that hang on either side of the body.
Group: Copepods
Size: Less than ¼ in (0.5 cm)
Distribution: Found throughout North America

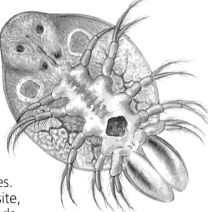

Fish Louse
(*Argulus* spp.)

This creature looks very different from the water louse (below). It has a flat body, a pair of suckers, and hooked appendages. The fish louse is a parasite, which means that it feeds and lives on another creature that is a "host." A louse clamps its suckers onto a host fish's body or fins and sucks up the fish's blood. The louse is also a good swimmer, kicking along in the water with its legs. Look closely at the gills and skin of a pike or other freshly caught fish, and you may spot a louse.
Group: Fish lice—Size: Up to ½ in (1 cm)
Distribution: Found throughout North America

Water Flea
(Order: Cladocera)

The entire body of these tiny crustaceans is enclosed in a transparent shell, leaving only the antennae and legs free. Water fleas swim by "rowing" with their antennae; they use their legs to take food particles from the water. Water fleas vary in color, from greenish to brown or red. They can be found in great numbers in many freshwater habitats, especially ponds.
Group: Water fleas
Size: Up to ¾ in (2 cm)
Distribution: Found throughout North America

Water Louse
(*Asellus aquaticus*)

This creature is a flattened version of the familiar wood louse that is found on land. The water louse can be found in almost all kinds of water, including puddles. It feeds on decaying plant and animal material. It is unable to swim, instead it crawls over mud and plants. In spring some ponds teem with thousands of these little animals.
Group: Isopods
Size: Up to ¾ in (2 cm)
Distribution: Found throughout North America

Chimney Crayfish
(Cambarus diogenes)

Crayfish look like miniature lobsters, but they live in fresh water instead of the sea. Many of them live in shallow streams, hidden under flat stones or in a shallow burrow. The chimney crayfish, however, is found in ponds, swamps, and meadows. In these habitats, it digs a burrow up to three feet (around 1 meter) deep, with a chamber at the bottom filled with water. At the top of the burrow, the crayfish often builds a turret or chimney several inches high.

Group: Crayfishes
Size: 2–6 in (5–15 cm)
Distribution: Found throughout the U.S. east of the Rockies

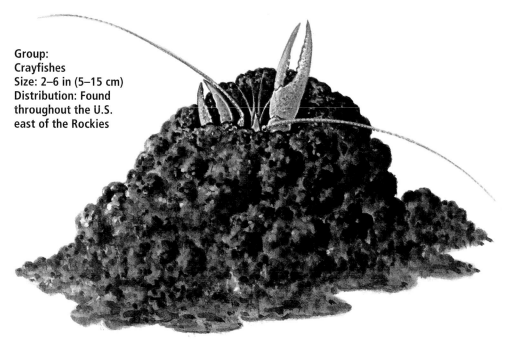

Fairy Shrimp
(Order: Anostraca)

These little creatures live in small, temporary pools—often in woodlands or old forests. They appear suddenly in spring when the water from melted snow and ice or rain fills potholes. Once hatched, they swim along upside down, using their 11 pairs of leaflike legs. This motion also brings them the water from which they filter food. Females lay eggs, which sink into the bottom mud. When the pool dries up, the eggs survive there, hatching when a fresh supply of water fills the pool.

Group: Fairy shrimps
Size: Up to 1¾ in (4.5 cm)
Distribution: Found throughout North America

Freshwater Prawn
(Family: Palaemonidae)

Most prawns and shrimps live in salt water, but freshwater prawns can survive in pools and ditches some distance away from the sea. Their newly hatched larvae migrate to salty water. They move slowly along the bottom, picking up bits of weed with their two pairs of pincers.

Group: Shrimps and prawns
Size: 1–1¼ in (2.5–3 cm)
Distribution: Found throughout North America

Ponds & Shallow Lakes

Whirligig Beetle Larva
(Family: Gyrinidae)

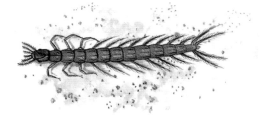

The young, or larvae, of the whirligig beetle look a lot like centipedes. Instead of many pairs of legs, however, it has only three. The rest of its "legs" are really gills. It hunts along the bottoms of ponds and streams for other insect larvae and plants to eat. You can tell this larva from the similar alderfly larva, because it does not have a pointed, hairy tail.
Group: Whirligig beetles—Size: Up to ¾ in (2 cm)
Distribution: Found throughout North America

Alderfly Larva
(Family: Sialidae)

Adult alderflies can be found hiding among plants by the water's edge. By contrast, the young alderfly lives in the water at the muddy bottoms of ponds, ditches, and streams. The larva has a long, brown body, with three pairs of legs and seven pairs of thin gills sticking out from it. The tail ends in a single hairy point. It is a hunter and catches its prey with strong pincerlike jaws.

Group: Alderflies
Size: About 1 in (2.5 cm)
Distribution: Found throughout North America

Dragonfly Nymph
(Order: Odonata)

The whirring wings and bright colors of adult dragonflies are a familiar sight around ponds and lakes. However, these beautiful insects start life as plain-looking, brown nymphs that live in the water. A dragonfly nymph is a ferocious hunter, using its hinged jaws (called a mask) to seize its prey. The nymph can swim by jet propulsion, pumping water in and out of its body.

Group: Dragonflies and damsel flies
Size: Up to 4 in (10 cm)
Distribution: Found throughout North America

Mosquito Larva
(Family: Culicidae)

Tiny, wriggling, wormlike mosquito larvae are a familiar sight in water barrels, gutters, and any stagnant water (water that is not moved by a current). Look at them through a magnifying glass, and you will see that each one has a round-shaped head. It breathes through a tube in its tail, which sticks out above the water's surface. You will sometimes find these larvae hanging upside-down at the surface of water in small ponds, ditches, bogs, and marshes. Luckily, they are a favorite food of fish, which helps keep their numbers down.

Group: Mosquitoes and gnats
Size: Up to ½ in (1 cm)
Distribution: Found throughout North America

Northern Caddisfly Larva

(Family: Limnephilidae)

If you ever see a bundle of twigs walking across the bottom of your collecting bucket, it is probably a caddisfly larva. The larva of the caddisfly looks like a caterpillar, if you can ever see it properly. The larva builds a special case to protect itself. The species shown will use anything available to make its case, from tiny sticks arranged in a crisscross pattern to snail shells and stones all stuck together by fine silk secreted by the larva. Look for these larva cases on the bottom while pond-dipping.

Group: Caddisflies
Size: Up to ¾ in (1.2 cm)
Distribution: Found throughout North America

Diving Beetle Larva

(Family: Dytiscidae)

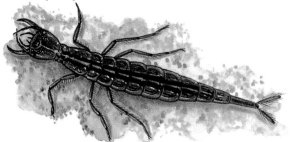

The adult diving beetle is a ferocious predator, but its larva is even worse! The larva can walk along the bottom mud, or swim, using its legs as oars. It will attack anything from tadpoles and insects to fish with its fierce, pincerlike jaws. **Watch out, as it can also give you a nasty nip.** This larva sticks its tail out of the water to take in air through special tubes.
Group: Beetles—Size: Up to 2¾ in (7 cm)
Distribution: Found throughout North America

Molanna Caddisfly Larva

(Family: Molannidae)

This type of caddisfly larva builds a different kind of case for its protection. It makes a net tube built out of sand—the net tube sits on a flat, sandy platform. This species can be found on the sandy bottoms of lakes or ponds, or in slow-flowing streams.
Group: Caddisflies
Size: Up to 1 in (2.5 cm)
Distribution: Found throughout North America

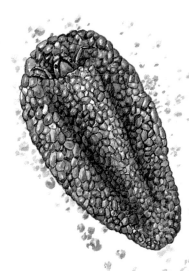

Damsel Fly Nymph

(Order: Odonata)

The adult damsel fly is like a small, slender version of the dragonfly. Its nymph, or young, is also more slender than that of the dragonfly nymph. It can easily be identified by the three leaflike gills at its tail end. It cannot propel itself as can the dragonfly nymph, but it hunts in a similar way, crawling about among the mud and weeds. Look for the empty "shells" of dragonfly and damsel fly nymphs, clinging to plants above the water's surface. These shells are left behind when the nymphs turn into flying adults.

Group:
Damsel flies
Size: Up to 3 in
(7.5 cm)
Distribution: Found
throughout North America

Hydra
(Hydra oligactis)

This tiny, brown creature looks more like a plant than an animal. Some hydras are green and look even more plantlike. The hydra has a slender body and about five to seven tentacles. When the hydra is hungry, it stretches these tentacles out to several times their normal length. They can sting and paralyze minute animals such as water fleas, which tumble into them. The hydra then pulls in its tentacles and pushes the food into its mouth. Hydras usually stay attached to water plants but can let go and drift in the water. Or, they can move slowly along by turning somersaults. Look on page 71 to discover how you can find and keep these animals.

Group: Hydroids—Size: Up to ½ in (1 cm)
Distribution: Found throughout North America

Freshwater Sponge
(Class: Demospongiae)

Most sponges live in the sea, but a few small ones survive in fresh water. A sponge does not look like an animal, but it is. Look for a soft, spongy mass attached to sunken branches, stones, and wooden pilings. The shape varies according to where it is living. It may be flat, rounded, or have fingerlike growths. It is usually greenish, but can be purple, or gray in areas with less light. Sponges feed and breathe by drawing water into themselves through tiny tunnels; they then filter food and extract oxygen from this water. They can be found only in clean water in ponds, lakes, rivers, and canals.

Group: Sponges—Size: Up to 8 in (20 cm)
Distribution: Found throughout North America

Medicinal Leech
(Hirudo medicinalis)

Leeches are types of worms that have muscular, stretchy bodies with a sucker at each end. The medicinal leech is greenish in color, with long stripes and bright orange spots in the middle. Its underside is rich orange in color and may have black spots. It sucks the blood of mammals, including humans, by first piercing the skin with its teeth-lined jaws. It then uses a special chemical that it produces to cause the host's blood to flow freely. This leech is called "medicinal" because it was often used for medical purposes in the past.

Group: Leeches
Size: Up to 8 in (20 cm)
Distribution: Found throughout North America

Horse Leech
(Haemopis sanguisuga)

This large leech lives in ponds or marshes, or it wanders about in damp places searching for food. It has a stout, flattened body that may be blackish-green to yellow-green or brown. The name is misleading, because it rarely sucks blood from horses or other large animals. More often, it eats small animals such as earthworms or even tadpoles. It swallows them whole, as it has weak jaws with few teeth.

Group: Leeches
Size: Up to 6 in (15 cm)
Distribution:
Found throughout
North America

Common Freshwater Leech
(Helobdella stagnalis)

This leech is one of many types of freshwater leech and is similar in shape to the snail leech, but it has a very soft body. It is pale gray, with a green, yellow, or brownish tinge. There is a tiny, hard scale on its back, but you will need to look very closely to see this! It lives in rivers, lakes, and ponds and feeds on snails.

Group: Leeches
Size: ¼–1¼ in (0.5–3 cm)
Distribution:
Found throughout
North America

Nasal Leech
(Theromyzon tessulatum)

This leech has a soft, almost jellylike, flattened body. It is amber or gray in color, and large specimens have rows of yellow stripes along the back. The underside is pale gray. It feeds by getting into the nasal passages and mouths of water birds, especially ducks, and sucking their blood. It does not swim.

Group: Leeches
Size: ½–1¼ in (1–3 cm)
Distribution:
Found throughout
North America

Snail Leech
(Glossiphonia complanata)

This leech has a ribbed, flattened, leaf-shaped body that is dull green to brownish in color. It has several rows of yellowish spots and two dark broken lines running along its back. As the name suggests, it feeds on snails. The snail leech leads an inactive life, spending much of its time hidden under stones. It is common in both still and running water.

Group: Leeches
Size: ½–1½ in (1–4 cm)
Distribution:
Found throughout
North America

Fish Leech
(Family: Piscicolidae)

As the name suggests, this leech feeds on fish. Its body is cylinder-shaped and may be colored green, yellow, or brown; it may also have white spots. When hungry, it "fishes" from a rock, waving about until a fish passes. Then it lets go and swims fast until it catches the fish and clamps tightly to the fish with its large suckers. After sucking the fish's blood, the leech lets go and hides among the plants. If you get one in your net, it will be easy to spot as it will curl rapidly about. These leeches are found wherever there are fish.

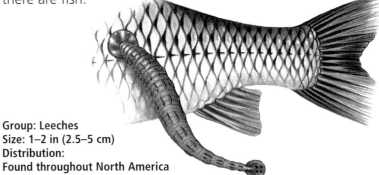

Group: Leeches
Size: 1–2 in (2.5–5 cm)
Distribution:
Found throughout North America

Keeping Tadpoles

Check with your teacher or an expert at a local nature center before doing these activities. The teacher or expert may recommend a different activity that will be more appropriate for your locality. Nature activities can be harmful to animals or their environment, or to you, so it always is best to get expert advice and to have an adult along on any expedition.

Collecting spawn and tadpoles

The best place to collect frog spawn (eggs) is from a garden pond. Only collect from a "wild" pond if an expert or teacher decides there is plenty there. Remember, it takes a great many tadpoles to produce just a few frogs, because so many tadpoles get eaten by predators.

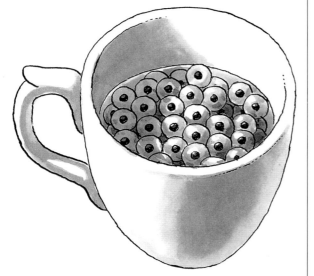

1 **Collect a few dozen tadpoles (or half a cup of spawn),** using a small aquarium net. (Frog spawn is somewhat easier to find.) Carry the tadpoles home in a small bucket.

2 **Put the tadpoles into a small aquarium tank** (see page 70). Add tap water that has stood outside for a day or two to get rid of the chlorine, or pond water if it is not too muddy.
3 **Add a few rocks and some water plants.** Cover the tank with netting to keep out predators.
4 **Place the tank in dappled shade.** Tadpoles like warm water, but may die if left in full sunshine.

5 **Your tadpoles will need to be fed a few days after they hatch,** unless you have a large tank with a lot of water plants. At this stage tadpoles are plant-eaters. Add small pieces of boiled lettuce leaves and four to five pellets of rabbit food to the tank every three or four days.
6 **Change the water if it gets murky and add more water as it evaporates.**

Total body change

1 **Watch your tadpoles carefully** and you will see them gradually change into adults. This change is called metamorphosis. Keep a diary of what happens.
   - Can you see the gills (salamanders only)?
   - Which comes first—hindlegs or front legs?
2 **When the hindlegs have appeared** (about five to six weeks after hatching), put some rocks or twigs in the tank for them to climb upon. The tadpoles will soon need to breathe air.
3 **Now they need to eat meat.** So give them small pieces of raw meat (like liver), about once a week. Remove uneaten food after a couple of days and change the water twice a week.
4 **When the front legs appear**, prop up the tank so that there is a shallow end. Or you can build some islands using rocks.
5 **These small frogs should be released** by the edge of the pond from which you took the spawn. They are very difficult to feed now, so it is better to let them go. Carry them in a box with damp moss or grass. They will drown in a bucket of water.

Swamps & Marshes

Also called wetlands, these habitats are neither water nor dry land. They are found mostly in lowland areas, especially where there is heavy rainfall or flooding. Wetlands that have trees growing in them are called swamps.

Bogs and marshes don't have trees. They develop in the shallows around lakes and ponds and at the edges of quiet streams. There is little water movement, so plants such as reeds, sedges, and water-loving grasses can grow out into the water.

Swamps, marshes, and bogs are ideal places for animals that like to spend only part of their time in the water, such as snakes and alligators. There are also pools in these habitats for permanent water animals such as fish. This picture shows several animals from this book—see how many you can identify.

Reptiles

American Crocodile
(Crocodylus acutus)

You can tell a crocodile from an American alligator by its pointed snout. The crocodile has dark bands on its back and tail. A crocodile's skin is tough and knobby. Its jaws are lined with sharp, peglike teeth, which it uses to seize prey such as crabs, fish, raccoons, and water birds. Even when its mouth is closed, some teeth are visible. The crocodile lives in bogs and mangrove swamps. Unfortunately, its survival is endangered by hunters and also by people destroying its natural habitat.
Group: Crocodiles—Size: 12 ft (3.7 m)
Distribution: Coast of southern Florida and the Florida Keys

Spectacled Caiman
(Caiman crocodilus)

A relative of the crocodile and alligator, the spectacled caiman is smaller than its kin. The caiman is colored light brown to light yellow, with bands on its back and tail. It gets the name "spectacled" from the bony ridge between its eyes, which looks like the frame of a pair of spectacles (glasses). The spectacled caiman lives in swamps, rivers, canals, and ponds, and it feeds on fish, small birds, mammals, and amphibians.
Group: Crocodiles—Size: 4–8½ ft (1.2–2.5 m)
Distribution: Introduced to southern Florida from Central and South America

American Alligator
(Alligator mississippiensis)

The alligator is the largest reptile in North America. Adults have thick, rough, knobby skin that is dull gray and dark olive in color. The alligator's snout is rounded, broad, and shovellike, a feature that helps distinguish it from the American crocodile. The alligator's jaws are lined with sharp teeth. It lives in marshes, ponds, lakes, rivers, and swamps, where it spends its time sunbathing on the banks, or swimming underwater with only the top of its head above the surface. It feeds on different animals, from fish and frogs to snakes and mammals. Alligators were once hunted by people for their hides, but they are now protected by law.

Group: Crocodiles—Size: Up to 12 ft (3.7 m)
Distribution: Southern Atlantic coast and coastal areas of the southern U.S.

Reptiles

Swamps & Marshes

Green Water Snake
(Nerodia cyclopion)

This snake is usually greenish or brownish in color. There are faint, broken bars in black on its sides. Underneath, its belly is cream to brown and may have spots. The green water snake lives in marshes, swamps, ditches, and canals—it is usually active by day, when it feeds on minnows and other small fish.
Group: Colubrid snakes—Size: 2½–6 ft (0.75–1.8 m)
Distribution: South, southeast, and south-central U.S.

Striped Crayfish Snake
(Regina alleni)

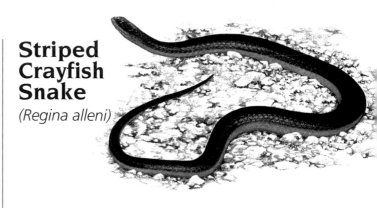

This snake's skin is quite glossy and brown, with a wide yellow or orange stripe running down its sides. There are also three faint dark stripes running down its back, and its belly is plain yellow to orange-brown. You will find this snake where there are water hyacinths growing, in swamps, ponds, and lakes. The striped crayfish snake's name gives a big clue to its diet, which is purely crayfish. It catches it prey by encircling the creature with its body—when the crayfish is unable to escape, the snake swallows it whole. Female striped crayfish snakes give birth to live young, sometime between May and September.
Group: Colubrid snakes
Size: 1–2 ft (0.3–0.6 m)
Distribution: Southern Georgia and the Florida peninsula in the U.S.

Water Moccasin
(Agkistrodon piscivorus)

Group: Pit vipers—Size: 3½–5 ft (1–1.5 m)
Distribution: Eastern, central, and southern U.S.
WARNING: Avoid—EXTREMELY POISONOUS!
This snake's bite can kill you.

Also called the cottonmouth, this is a large water snake with a flat-topped head that is wider than its neck. The snake can be olive, brown, or black in color, and can be plainly patterned or have dark bands on its sides. Young water moccasins have strong markings and bright yellow tails. This snake lives mainly in swamps, lakes, rivers, and ditches, but can even be found in mountain streams. It swims along with its head out of the water and can sometimes be seen basking on banks. It becomes most active at night, when it hunts frogs, fish, snakes, and birds. When threatened, the snake raises its head and opens its white-lined mouth. **Keep away!**

Swamp Snake
(Seminatrix pygaea)

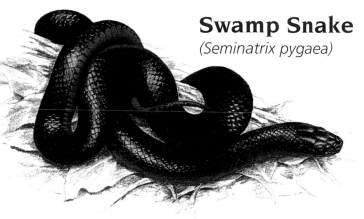

The swamp snake has a glossy, black skin with a red belly. The black color extends to the edges of the belly scales, giving an attractive pattern of triangles on either side of the belly. As the name suggests, this snake likes to live in swamps, especially where water hyacinths grow in large numbers. It can often be seen hiding among these plants, or it might be seen at night in the open after a heavy rainfall. The swamp snake feeds on leeches, small fish, frogs, and tadpoles. The females give birth to live young.
Group: Colubrid snakes
Size: Nearly 1–1½ ft (0.3–0.5 m)
Distribution: Coastal regions of the southern and eastern U.S.

Plain-bellied Water Snake
(Nerodia erythrogaster)

This snake is so called because its belly is always plain red, orange, or yellow. The rest of the body is reddish-brown, greenish, or gray, and it is covered in rough scales. This water snake can be seen in river swamps and on the wooded edges of streams, ponds, and lakes. It feeds on frogs, fish, tadpoles, and crayfish. Look for it in the early evening, as this is when it becomes most active. You may see it crossing a road on a rainy night.
Group: Colubrid snakes—Size: 2½–5 ft (0.75–1.5 m)
Distribution: Eastern and southern, and some parts of the midwestern U.S.

Rainbow Snake
(Farancia erytrogramma)

This snake is called the rainbow snake because of the rainbow of red, yellow, and black stripes on its body. Its belly is red with a double row of black spots. The tail has a sharp—but harmless—spine on the end. The rainbow snake burrows into sandy soil or under wet plants on the edge of streams and rivers. It comes out mainly at night, but it may be seen during the day hunting for eels, its favorite food.
Group: Colubrid snakes
Size: 3–5½ ft (1–1.6 m)
Distribution: East Coast and southern regions of the U.S.

Deep & Cold Waters

Lakes vary a lot in size and depth. For some animals the size of their home is important. There are a number of fish, amphibians, and reptiles that live only in large, and usually deep, lakes and rivers. The alligator snapping turtle and a fish called the burbot are some examples.

Other animals will live only in cold waters. This means they are found only in northern areas, where water temperatures in large lakes and rivers remain low all the year around. This picture shows several animals from this book—see how many you can identify.

48

Pacific Giant Salamander
(Dicamptodon tenebrosus)

This large, fat-bodied salamander has smooth skin, with black marbling over a brown or purplish base. Its belly is light brown or yellowish-white. The adult Pacific giant salamander can be found under logs or rocks in cool, damp forests, or by clear, cold rivers and streams. Like most salamanders, in the larva stage giants have gills and live in the water, where they eat tadpoles and insects. Adults eat larger insects, mice, other salamanders, and small snakes.

Group: Mole salamanders
Size: 7–12 in (18–30 cm)
Distribution: Northern Pacific coast of Canada and the U.S., and some areas of the Rocky Mountains in the U.S.

Mink Frog
(Rana septentrionalis)

Spotted Frog
(Rana pretiosa)

This large frog is brown, with irregular, dark spots. It has a light stripe on its upper jaw. Its belly is yellow, orange, or red, with darker mottling on the throat. The spotted frog lives near cold mountain streams, rivers, and lakes and is active during the day. Its voice sounds like a series of short croaks.

Group: True frogs
Size: 2–4 in (5–10 cm)
Distribution: Northwestern regions of North America

This frog is so called because of the musky odor it gives off when threatened or handled. It is olive or brown, with dark patches on its sides and hind legs. Its belly is somewhat yellow. This frog lives in cold northern ponds or lakes, especially those with water lilies. During the night, when this frog is most active, it often can be seen sitting on a lily pad, croaking in a low-pitched tone.

Group: True frogs
Size: 2–3 in (5–7.5 cm)
Distribution: Eastern Canada and the northeastern U.S.

Deep & Cold Waters

Lake Chub
(Couesius plumbeus)

This fish is a type of minnow. It is slender with a short head, large eyes, and a rounded snout. There are little barbels ("whiskers") on either side of its mouth. Its body is brown above, and silvery or white underneath, with a darker line running along the sides. The lake chub lives in cold lakes and small streams, where it feeds on insect larvae.

Group: Carps and minnows
Size: Up to 4 in (10 cm)
Distribution: Found throughout Canada and in the northern and midwestern regions of the U.S.

Alligator Snapping Turtle
(Macroclemys temminckii)

This huge, fearsome-looking creature is the largest freshwater turtle in North America! It has a dark brown shell with three rows of knobs and a jagged edge. It also has a very long tail and a big head with a dangerous-looking, hooked beak. If it opens its mouth, it reveals a pink, wormlike appendage that acts like a fishing lure, attracting prey to the turtle's mouth. These turtles live in deep rivers and large lakes. You may find it difficult to spot a snapping turtle, as these animals spend most of their time sitting at the bottom of the water, open-mouthed, hoping to attract prey. It will eat anything it can swallow and **can give a serious wound to humans.**

Group: Snapping turtles
Size: Over 24 in (60 cm)
Distribution: Southern and midwestern regions of the U.S.
BEWARE—this animal can give you a serious injury if it bites you!

Map Turtle

(Graptemys geographica)
This turtle gets its name from the pattern on its shell. The shell is flattened and greenish-brown, with thin yellow-orange lines that look like the markings for rivers or paths on a map. The undershell is yellowish. The head and limbs are greenish with narrow, yellow stripes. Females have much bigger heads than males and can feed on freshwater clams and snails as a result. Males and youngsters eat mainly insects and crayfish. The map turtle lives in large, slow-flowing rivers and lakes with muddy bottoms and a lot of plants and logs. Look for logs where groups of map turtles may be sitting one on top of another, basking in the sunshine.

Group: Pond and marsh turtles—Size: 4–12 in (10–30 cm)
Distribution: Eastern central U.S.

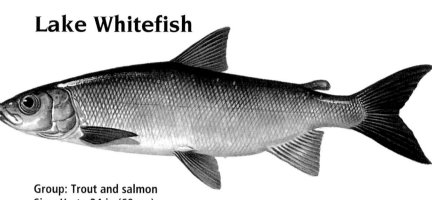

(Coregonus clupeaformis)
This slender, silvery-green fish looks very much like the herring found in the sea. It really belongs to the trout family, however—like other trout, it has a small, fleshy, second (adipose) fin on its back. It has a small conical head and mouth and a forked tail. As its name suggests, the lake whitefish mostly lives in lakes, but it can also be found in wide, slow rivers. Large numbers of this fish are caught in nets by commercial fishers. If they escape the nets, whitefish can live for over 20 years. They eat insects and shellfish and typically live in deep water.

Lake Whitefish

Group: Trout and salmon
Size: Up to 24 in (60 cm)
Distribution: Found in most of Canada and in Alaska and northern U.S.

Group: Trout and salmon
Size: Up to 12 in (30 cm)
Distribution: Northern, central, and eastern U.S. and most of Canada

Lake Cisco
(Coregonus artedii)

You may find it hard to tell the lake cisco from the lake whitefish because they are very similar. In fact, even the experts can't agree on how many different sorts of whitefish and ciscoes there are! The lake cisco, also called the lake herring, has a lower jaw slightly longer than its upper, whereas, the size is reversed in the lake whitefish. The lake cisco eats mainly plankton, crustaceans, and insect larvae. In turn, it is eaten by bigger fish and by people.

Lake Trout
(Salvelinus namaycush)

Group: Trout and salmon
Size: 24 in (60 cm)
Distribution: Canada and Alaska, Great Lakes, and northeastern regions of the U.S.

Most trout, like those on pages 62–63, live in fast flowing streams and rivers. The lake trout prefers deep, cold lakes and rivers. Long and slender, this large fish has a gray-green body covered with white spots and a forked tail fin. Young fish feed on insects and crustaceans; when they get older, they feed on fish such as ciscoes. Females lay their eggs in the autumn in a shallow nest called a redd. The female scoops out the redd with her tail.

Deep & Cold Waters

Emerald Shiner

(Notropis atherinoides)

This little fish is a type of minnow and gets its name from its shiny scales and the green stripe that runs along its sides. The rest of its slender body is silvery-white. Its tail fin is forked and its back fin is transparent. The emerald shiner lives in lakes and large rivers, often in huge shoals. It feeds mainly on tiny floating plants, and animals called plankton. It is often used as bait by anglers.
Group: Carps and minnows
Size: Up to 4 in (10 cm)
Distribution: Found throughout Canada into the central U.S.

Longnose Sucker

(Catostomus catostomus)

The longnose sucker is so called because of the long, rounded snout that hangs over its lower lip. It is mostly a dark, mottled brown color, with a silvery-white underside. During the breeding season, males have a bright red stripe along the sides. This fish lives mostly in the clear, cold waters of deep lakes and rivers, where it feeds on plant material and small animals. Females lay eggs in the late spring that stick to the bottom gravel.

Group:
Suckers
Size: Up to 24 in (60 cm)
Distribution: East of the Rocky Mountains in Canada and the far northern U.S.

Brook Stickleback

(Culaea inconstans)

This fish is easily recognized from the five to seven short, backward-pointing spines on its back. Like the more familiar three-spined stickleback (see page 14), it has no scales on its body. Its tail fin is rounded. The brook stickleback is brownish-green, with lighter coloring on its belly, which also features another spine. It lives in the cool, clear waters of northern lakes and streams and feeds on small crustaceans and insects. The male builds a nest in spring, which he guards fiercely once the female has laid her eggs.
Group: Sticklebacks—Size: 1–4 in (2.5–10 cm)
Distribution: North-central and northeast U.S., and most of Canada

Burbot

(Lota lota)

This is a strange-looking fish. Its body is long, almost eel-shaped, with fins that run along the back and underneath. There is a small barbel (see catfish, page 28) under its chin, which looks rather like a beard. The burbot is usually mottled brown and yellowish, but color is variable. It lives in large, cold rivers and lakes. It has a big appetite and feeds mainly at dusk and dawn on fish, crayfish, and other water animals. It breeds in the winter, under the ice if its lake is frozen.
Group: Cod fishes—Size: Up to 36 in (90 cm)
Distribution: Canada and Alaska and central regions of the U.S.

Walleye

(Stizostedion vitreum vitreum)

Group: Darters and perches
Size: 12–36 in (30–90 cm)
Distribution: Northern and central U.S., and Canada

The walleye belongs to the same group of fish as the perch and also has a forked tail and two back fins. The first back fin has spines. It has a much longer body than the perch, however. The walleye has large glassy eyes. Its body is an olive-green color, with several narrow, dark bands across the back. Its tail has dark markings on it. The walleye lives in large streams, rivers, lakes, and reservoirs, as long as they flow over sandy or rocky bottoms. It feeds mainly on other fish and breeds in the spring in shallower waters.

Yellow Perch

(Perca flavescens)

This fish can be recognized by its golden-yellow body, which has six to eight dark bars running vertically. Its tigerlike coloration has given it another name, the tiger trout. Scales are easy to see on its body. The first of its two back fins has spines, as does the fin underneath its body. Its tail fin is forked. The yellow perch lives in large, clear streams, lakes, and reservoirs which have plant life. It swims around in groups, feeding on insects, snails, and other fish. Females lay eggs in a ribbonlike string embedded in a jellylike substance. These strings sometimes contain as many as 80,000 eggs!

Group: Darters and perches
Size: 5–12 in (12.5–30 cm)
Distribution: Eastern Canada and most of the U.S., east of the Rockies; introduced elsewhere

White Bass

(Morone chrysops)

This fish is plump-bodied and silvery in color, with six or seven dark stripes running along its sides from head to tail. The scales are medium in size. It has two fins on its back, the first fin has spines. There are also spines on the fin underneath its body and another on the gill cover. Its lower jaw protrudes beyond its upper jaw. The white bass lives in lakes and large, clear rivers that flow over gravel or rubble (rock). Females lay eggs in late spring or early summer—these eggs settle onto the gravel bottoms. White bass swim in big groups and feed on small fish.

Group: Bass—**Size:** Up to 15 in (38 cm)
Distribution: Southern Great Lakes and Mississippi River Valley to Florida in the U.S.

Collecting & Sampling

Make a minnow trap

An easy way to study fish is to catch and observe them. This trap should catch minnows, darters, or catfish. Move the trap gently and release the fish after you observe them.

1 **Make two cone shapes** out of large wire mesh.
2 **Fix the wide end of each cone** on to a circle of heavy wire.
3 **Push the narrow ends back inside** to make two smaller cones pointing inward.

4 **Cut the ends off the small cones to leave a small hole** big enough for small fish to swim through (about 2–3 inches [5–7.5 centimeters] across). **Ask an adult to help you with wire cutters.**
5 **Fix the two halves together** with a wire hinge and clip so the trap can be easily opened.
6 **Bait the trap** with dry dog or cat food or scraps of meat and fish. Put the bait in a fine mesh bag and hang it inside the trap.
7 **Set the trap some way out in a pond, lake, or stream.** Let it drift downstream from a dock, for example.
8 **Anchor it with a rope** to a dock or to a bush or tree and leave it for several hours or overnight.
9 **Don't forget to check it the next day** or the trapped fish will die.

Check with your teacher or an expert at a nature center before doing these activities. That adult may recommend a different activity that will be more appropriate for your locality. Nature activities can be harmful to animals or their environment, or to you, so it always is best to get expert advice and to have an adult along on any expedition.

Stream-bottom sampler

A trap placed in a fast-flowing stream is ideal for catching the animals that live there.

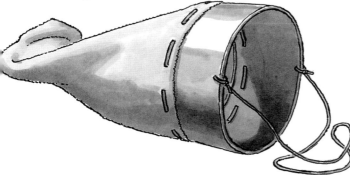

1 **Ask an adult to help you remove the bottom from a large cookie tin.**
2 **Take a conical net** (you can purchase one from a sporting-goods store) **and punch small holes** (that match up) into both the net and the tin. Attach the tin to the net with heavy string, and make a string handle (as shown) on the top of the tin.

3 **Plant a stick in the stream. (Ask an adult to help.)** Put the "handle" of the tin over the stick, and place the open mouth of the tin facing upstream.
4 **Use a second stick to stir up the bottom sediment** toward the trap. Animals will be dislodged and will be swept into the net.

Pollution Watch

Is your local pond, lake, river, or stream polluted? Here are some of the signs to look for:

- **Water changes color or is cloudy** (except after heavy rain)
- **Metal garbage**: like shopping carts or baby carriages
- **Sewage**: disposable diapers, toilet paper, etc.
- **Thick, green algae** covering the surface— this can be a sign of nitrogen pollution
- **Bad smells** coming from the water
- **White or brown foam** on the surface— possibly from a factory spill
- **A line of grease** on rocks and boulders above the usual water level
- **Oil or gas spills**—these show up as rainbow-colored circles floating on the surface
- **Dead fish** floating in the river or washed up in the shallows (unless this is an explained event, such as the alewife die-off that occurs during certain seasons in the Great Lakes region)

If there is a marked change in the body of water you monitor, alert an adult as soon as you can and ask her or him to inform the local health officials.

Fast Streams & Rivers

Many rivers begin life far up in the hills or mountains. Swift currents run over boulders, stones, and gravel, sweeping away mud or sand from the riverbed. On steep downhill sections there may be waterfalls or rapids. The rushing water provides plenty of oxygen, but the animals living here must be strong enough to prevent being washed away in the current.

Many insect larvae can live here. Some caddisfly larvae spin silken nets between rocks to catch their food. Black fly larvae often use tiny hooks at their tail ends to anchor themselves to wet boulders. Look also for the dusky salamander and the two-lined salamander that feed on the insect larvae hiding beneath stones.

Few snails are found in fast waters, but pearl mussels fix themselves to the stream bed and rely on the current to bring them food. Crayfish cling to the sides of rocks with their strong legs and claws.

Small fish such as sculpins are flattened on their lower side and so are streamlined..They lie with their head pointing upstream so that the water flows over them. Trout and salmon are also streamlined and are powerful swimmers. This picture shows many animals from this book—see how many you can identify.

Amphibians

Fast Streams & Rivers

Tailed Frog
(Ascaphus truei)

This frog gets its name from its "tail," which is only present in males. The tailed frog is colored olive, gray, or black, with a lot of dark spots and some small bumps on its back. Usually, a dark stripe runs from the snout through the eye, and the snout itself has a yellowish triangle. The tailed frog lives in cold, clear, fast-flowing mountain streams, or in nearby damp forests. Its tadpoles have sucking mouthparts that help them cling to rocks and logs in strong currents. Unlike most other frogs, this one does not make any sound.

Group: Tailed frogs—Size: 1–2 in (2.5–5 cm)
Distribution: Northern Pacific coast of Canada and the U.S.

Cascades Frog

(Rana cascadae)
This frog can be recognized by the inky-black spots on its brown to olive-brown back. It has a dark patch covering the eye and eardrum, a light jaw stripe, and a yellow belly. This mountain frog lives near small streams, ponds, and lakes. You may see it in the water or hiding in the grass. The Cascades frog is active by day and makes a sound like the twang of a loose banjo string.

Group: True frogs—Size: 1¾–2¼ in (4.5–5.5 cm)
Distribution: Olympic and Cascade mountains of the northwestern U.S.

Hellbender
(Cryptobranchus alleganiensis)

This strange-looking creature is, in fact, quite harmless. Also called the devil dog, it is a giant salamander that never leaves the water. It looks slightly squashed and has a flattened tail. It seems to be too small for its skin, which is loose and wrinkled. Most hellbenders are gray or olive-brown with a lighter-colored belly. Some have spots and blotches. It lives in clear streams and rivers. You can find it by searching under rocks, where it likes to hide. It feeds on crayfish, snails, and worms.

Group: Giant salamanders—Size: 12–30 in (30–75 cm)
Distribution: Eastern, southern, and central U.S.

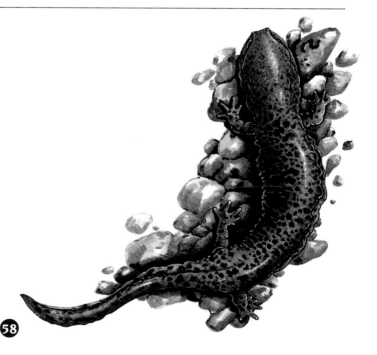

Foothill Yellow-legged Frog
(Rana boylii)

Group: True frogs
Size: 1–3 in (2.5–7.5 cm)
Distribution: Pacific region
of the U.S.

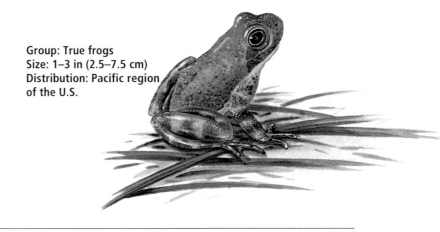

This frog is gray, brown, olive, or reddish in color, and usually has a mottled pattern. It gets its name from the yellow underside of its legs. It likes to live in gravel- or sand-bottomed streams that have sunny banks for basking and nearby woodlands. It is active mainly by day and makes a grating sound, but this is rarely heard.

Dusky Salamander
(Desmognathus fuscus)

This salamander is tan or dark brown and may have mottling on its body. Young salamanders of this type have several pairs of yellowish or reddish spots running down the back. The tail is triangular in shape. You will find the dusky salamander near rocky woodland creeks and streams, where the rocks provide shelter. It feeds on insect larvae, insects, and earthworms.

Group: Lungless
salamanders
Size: 2½–5½ in (6.5–14 cm)
Distribution: Southeastern Canada through the
southern region of the U.S.

Red Salamander
(Pseudotriton ruber)

Group: Lungless salamanders
Size: 2½–6 in (6.5–15 cm)
Distribution: Southeastern Canada through the southern
region of the U.S.

This stocky salamander is easy to spot, with its short tail, bright red coloring, and black spots. Older animals may become purplish-brown. If you get close, you will see that it has yellow eyes. The smaller mud salamander (see page 73) has brown eyes. The red salamander lives in and near springs, streams, cool brooks, and nearby woodland areas. It may wander some distance from the water, and it may hide in woodland leaf litter, or under rocks and stones.

Amphibians

Fast Streams & Rivers

Northern Two-lined Salamander
(Eurycea bislineata)

It's easy to see how this salamander gets its name. It has two dark lines bordering a broad, light stripe that runs right down its back. The broad stripe may be yellow, brown, green, or orange-bronze. The two-lined salamander lives by rock-bottomed brooks and springs and in river swamps and damp forests. It hides under rocks and leaf litter—if alarmed it will run or swim away.

Group: Lungless salamanders
Size: 2–5 in (5–12.5 cm)
Distribution: Southeastern Canada and the eastern U.S.

Olympic Salamander
(Rhyacotriton olympicus)

This small salamander is plain brown or mottled olive in color. It has a small head with bulging eyes, a slender body, and a short tail. Underneath, its belly is yellow-green or yellow-orange, with black flecks. The Olympic salamander lives in cold, fast-moving streams and springs near forests. When on land, it hides under stones. Its favorite foods include insects and spiders.

Group: Mole salamanders
Size: 3–5 in (7.5–12.5 cm)
Distribution: West coast of the U.S., especially the Olympic Peninsula in Washington

Long-tailed Salamander
(Eurycea longicauda)

Group: Lungless salamanders
Size: 4–8 in (10–20 cm)
Distribution: Eastern and central U.S.

One of the first things to notice about this salamander is its extremely long tail, which is slender and much longer than its body. The body is yellow to bright orange-red and is scattered with black spots that turn into bars on the tail. The long-tailed salamander likes to live by streams and springs near woodlands. On warm, rainy nights it may be seen on the forest floor searching for food.

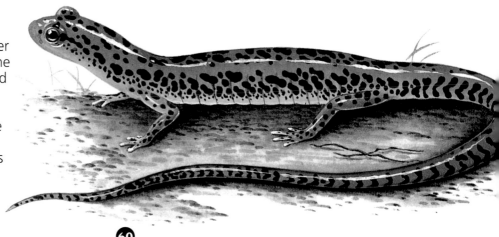

Black-bellied Salamander
(Desmognathus quadramaculatus)

Group: Lungless salamanders
Size: 3½–8 in (9–20 cm)
Distribution: Southern U.S.

This fat-bodied salamander is black with greenish blotches on its back. It is black-bellied, just as its name says. It likes fast-flowing mountain streams that have boulders for sunbathing. It rarely ventures far from the water's edge. Mainly active at night, the black-bellied salamander feeds on insects, snails, and smaller salamanders.

Spring Salamander
(Gyrinophilus porphyriticus)

Group: Lungless salamanders
Size: 4–9 in (10–23 cm)
Distribution: Southern Canada through the southern U.S.

This large salamander may be colored salmon-pink, brownish-pink, or red. Hazy, darker markings on top of this base color give it a pattern. A light bar runs from its eye to its nostril. Called the spring salamander because it prefers cool springs, you may also spot this salamander in mountain streams or beneath logs or stones in surrounding woodlands.

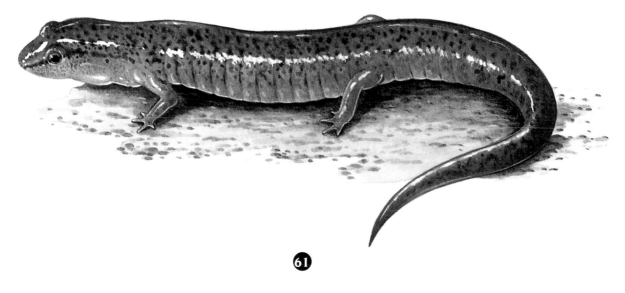

Atlantic Salmon
(Salmo salar)

Salmon and trout may be recognized by their streamlined shape and small, fleshy second back fin. You can tell them apart by their tails—most salmon have a slightly forked tail, whereas in trout, the tail is almost straight. Adult Atlantic salmon are silvery with a few scattered spots (see below). During the breeding season, the male develops red spots and a reddish belly. The Atlantic salmon has a complex life cycle. It spends most of its life in the sea, but at breeding time it returns to the stream in which it was hatched. Salmon will struggle up waterfalls and rapids to get there. After spawning, some die, but many return to the sea and later spawn again. The young, or parr, are quite dark and have blotchy sides. At 2 to 6 years of age, they start to move downstream, become silvery, and are called smolts.
Group: Trout and salmon
Size: 30 in (75 cm)
Distribution: North Atlantic and coastal waters of Canada and the U.S.

Rainbow Trout
(Oncorhynchus mykiss)

This fish gets its name from the beautiful red band along each side (see above). The body, tail, and back fin are also heavily speckled with small, dense black spots. Rainbow trout live mostly in clear, upland stream pools and in lakes. However, some rainbow trout live in the ocean. These trout are called steelheads, and they eventually return from the sea to breed in inland rivers and streams. The rainbow trout is sought after by anglers.
Group: Trout and salmon
Size: 40–45 in (100–110 cm)
Distribution: Native to the Pacific coast, introduced into Canada and the eastern U.S.

Brook Trout
(Salvelinus fontinalis)

The beautiful brook trout, or brook charr, can be recognized by its olive-green body, which is covered with wormlike patterns. Red spots surrounded by blue are scattered on its sides. The fins underneath its body are pink, edged with white, and males often have orange bellies in the autumn during the breeding season. Its tail fin is a squarish shape, which is why it is sometimes given the common name of squaretail. The brook trout prefers to live in cold, clear streams.

Group: Trout and salmon
Size: Up to 20 in (51 cm)
Distribution: Eastern Canada, and eastern, southern, and Great Lakes regions of the U.S.

Coho Salmon
(Oncorhynchus kisutch)

Another name for this fish is the hooknose—can you see why? Only the breeding males develop the hooked jaws and the red coloring along the sides. Its usual color is silvery with scattered, small black spots on its back and on the top of the tail. Like the Atlantic salmon, the young fish migrate downriver to live in the sea, but they do not go far offshore. They return upriver to spawn when they are 3 or 4 years old, swimming tirelessly until they get to the small headstreams. After spawning they all die—for a short time after, the streams are choked with their bodies.

Group: Trout and salmon
Size: 24 in (60 cm)
Distribution: Pacific Ocean (and rivers joining it) of Canada and the U.S., introduced to the Great Lakes

Brown Trout
(Salmo trutta)

This trout is greenish-brown with silvery sides and is speckled with large, dark spots. It also has scattered red spots faintly surrounded by blue. Unlike the rainbow trout, it has an unspotted tail. The brown trout lives in moderately fast rivers and streams, often hiding in quiet pools. However, like the rainbow trout, some brown trout migrate to the sea; then they are called sea trout. Brown trout become most active at dusk, when they "rise" to snap up surface insects. They also feed on mollusks, crustaceans, and even on smaller brown trout.

Group: Trout and salmon
Size: 10 in (25.5 cm)
Distribution: Introduced to North America from Europe and Asia; now widely found in Canada and the U.S.

Fast Streams & Rivers

Central Stoneroller
(Campostoma anomalum)

This fish is slender with a slightly hump-backed appearance. It is brownish on top and silvery-white underneath. The dark scales scattered over its back and sides can be easily spotted. There is a single fin on its back. Its snout overhangs its mouth, which gives the fish a bad-tempered appearance. The stoneroller gets its name from its behavior—rolling stones and gravel on the bottom of the streams, both to find food such as insect larvae and mollusks and to dig its nest in the spring.

Group: Carps and minnows
Size: Up to 8 in (20 cm)
Distribution: Southern Canada through most of the central and eastern U.S.

Brassy Minnow
(Hybognathus hankinsoni)

This little fish gets its name from its brassy-yellow sides, which glitter in the sunshine. The brassy minnow is slender, with a single fin on its back and a forked tail fin. Its medium-sized scales are easy to see. It lives in small, weedy creeks, where it creeps along the bottom searching for food in the mud. It lives in big groups, or "schools," and breeds in the spring.

Group: Carps and minnows
Size: Up to 4 in (10 cm)
Distribution: Eastern and central U.S. and southern Canada

Prickly Sculpin
(Cottus asper)

This sculpin is dark colored on top and lighter underneath. There are two fins on its back that merge into one; the first fin is spiny. Like other sculpins, this one has very big, wavy fins on its sides (pectoral fins). It lives in the quiet areas of coastal streams and spends most of its time hiding, only coming out to catch small animals to eat.

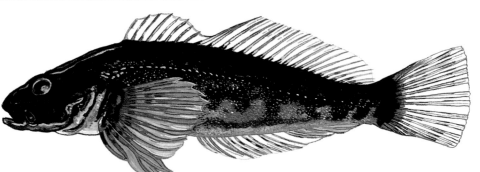

Group: Sculpins
Size: 3–4 in (7.5–10 cm)
Distribution: Northern Pacific Coast of North America

Mottled Sculpin
(Cottus bairdi)

Like most sculpins, this strange-looking fish has a large, flattened head and a large mouth. It has a rather lumpy appearance. As its name suggests, it is mottled, with brown, black, and gray markings. Its eyes are on top of its head, and its body has no scales. There are two large fins on its back; the first fin is black and spiny. The mottled sculpin lives in clear, cold streams, rivers, and lakes over rocky and gravel bottoms.

Group: Sculpins
Size: Up to 4 in (10 cm)
Distribution: All of southern Canada and most of the central and western U.S.

Longnose Dace
(Rhinichthys cataractae)

Named after the snout, which extends well past its mouth, the longnose dace is a long, slender fish. Its body is mottled with black and brown markings, and its underside is cream-colored. There is a single fin on its back, and its tail fin is slightly forked. This fish lives in schools, inhabiting swift-flowing streams and rivers that have gravelly bottoms. It feeds on small insects.
Group: Carps and minnows
Size: Up to 7 in (18 cm)
Distribution: Canada and most of the U.S. east of the Rockies

Slimy Sculpin
(Cottus cognatus)

This little fish has a slender, scaleless body that is greenish on top and creamy-yellow underneath. Its fins are pale gray in color. Two long, back fins almost merge into one; the first fin has seven weak spines. The slimy sculpin lives in deep, cool lakes and fast-flowing rivers and streams that have gravel and rocks on the bottom. In late spring, males dig a hollow under rocks and stones, then they use elaborate courtship displays to entice females to lay eggs there. The female goes into the nest and lays her sticky eggs on the undersides of the rocks.

Group: Sculpins
Size: Up to 4 in (10 cm)
Distribution: Canada, Alaska, and much of the continental U.S.

Fast Streams & Rivers

Creek Chub
(Semotilus atromaculatus)

The creek chub's body is long, slender, and colored bluish on top and silver underneath. A broad, dark band runs along each side from the snout to the beginning of the tail. There is one fin on the back and the tail fin is forked. There is a dark spot at the base of the back fin. The chub has a large mouth and a pointed snout that extends over the lower jaw. The creek chub lives in small, fast brooks and streams that flow over gravel, sand, or rocks. It feeds on insects, worms, and small fish.

Group: Carps and minnows
Size: Up to 12 in (30 cm)
Distribution: Found throughout most of the U.S. east of the Rockies

Smallmouth Bass
(Micropterus dolomieui)

Group: Sunfishes
Size: Up to 24 in (60 cm)
Distribution: Southeastern Canada and eastern, central, and southern U.S.

This fish has a stout, olive-brown to bronze body. It is so called because its mouth is not as big as in other types of bass. Its back fin is in two parts, the first jagged and spiny, the second soft-rayed. The smallmouth bass prefers to live in clear, mountain lakes and streams with rocky bottoms, where it feeds on insect larvae, crayfish, and fish. In the spring or summer, the male digs out a nest in the bottom gravel and then entices a female to lay eggs in it. Bass is a favorite with anglers.

Brook Silverside
(Labidesthes sicculus)

A slender body that looks shiny and transparent, and a small, pointed head are the trademarks of this fish. It is yellowish in color, with a silvery band along its sides. Underneath, it is silvery-white. There are two fins on its back, and the tail fin is forked. The brook silverside lives in calm areas of streams, rivers, and lakes that are full of plant growth. It feeds on insects from the water surface. In fact, it spends most of its time near the water surface and sometimes can be seen leaping out of the water.

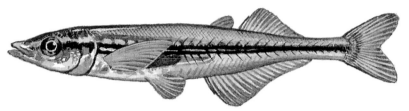

Group: Silverside
Size: Up to 4 in (10 cm)
Distribution: Found in most central and eastern states in the U.S.

Sailfin Molly
(Poecilia latipinna)

One look at this beautiful fish will tell you the reason for its name. It has a huge fin on its back that looks something like a sail on a boat. The body is not typically fish-shaped, as it is rather wide for its entire length. It is olive-brown in color with rows of colored spots. The tail fin is rounded, with a black margin. Males have much brighter colors and larger fins than females. The sailfin molly lives in fresh and brackish (fresh and salt) water areas of estuaries, swamps, and streams. Females give birth to live young instead of laying eggs. These fish are often kept in aquariums.
Group: Live bearers
Size: 3–6 in (7.5–15 cm)
Distribution: Coastal regions of the southeastern U.S. and Mexico

Rainbow Darter
(Etheostoma caeruleum)

The blue, green, orange, and red colors on the body of the males of this species earned the fish the name "rainbow darter." It has a fairly stout body with a large head and a blunt snout. There are two fins on its back; the first is spiny and the second has soft rays and is higher than the first. Its tail fin is long and square in shape. The rainbow darter swims in clear, cool streams and small rivers that flow over gravel. It feeds on small water insects, snails, and small crayfish.

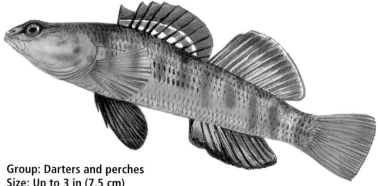

Group: Darters and perches
Size: Up to 3 in (7.5 cm)
Distribution: Southern Canada and central, southern, and eastern U.S.

Other Animals

Fast Streams & Rivers

Black Fly Larva
(Family: Simuliidae)

Swarms of tiny, biting black flies can be enough to spoil a summer picnic. The larvae of these annoying insects can cover the rocks and plants in a small, fast-flowing stream. Look carefully at the tops of rocks and around waterfalls, and you may see them. They fix themselves to the rock or plant by forming tiny hooks at their tail end. They strain food from the water with two foldable fans of bristles.

Group: Black flies
Size: Up to ¼ in (0.5 cm)
Distribution: Found throughout North America

Stonefly Nymph
(Order: Plecoptera)

Like many other insects that dwell near water, the stonefly hatches out of its egg as a nymph that lives underwater. Also known as creepers, these nymphs have strong legs for clinging beneath stones in the fast currents of streams, in which most of the species live. A pair of long antennae and two cerci, which are taillike feelers on the last segment of the abdomen, will help you to distinguish stonefly from May fly nymphs (see opposite), with which they are often found. Although usually plain brown, some species have beautiful patterns.

Group: Stoneflies—Size: Up to 1 in (2.5 cm)
Distribution: Found throughout North America

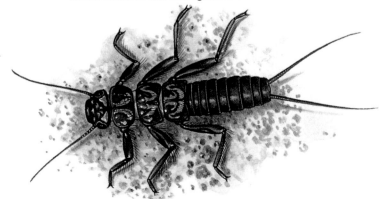

Caddisfly Larva

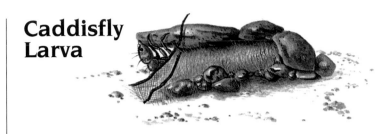

(Order: Trichoptera)
Most caddisfly larvae build themselves a case of twigs or stones to live in. (Find out how to observe this process on page 71.) The larva shown here acts much like a spider. Instead of forming a case, it spins a net of "silk" under or between rocks in a stream. Small animals are swept into it and eaten. If you look down into a clear stream, you might see crescent-shaped objects on the stream bed. These are entrances to the larvae's silken nets. These larvae live in fast-running waters.

Group: Caddisflies—Size: Up to ¾ in (2 cm)
Distribution: Found throughout North America

Mayfly Nymph
(Order: Ephemeroptera)

There are many different kinds of May flies, but all of them live near water. The nymphs, or young, live underwater—mostly in streams, rivers, and large lakes. Although different species vary in size and shape, all May fly nymphs have a row of either feathery or platelike gills along the sides of the body. Most have three thin cerci, which are taillike feelers on the last segment of the abdomen. Most May fly nymphs are brownish in color. The one shown here has short, sturdy legs and burrows into gravelly mud. Others cling beneath stones along with stonefly nymphs.

Group: Mayflies—Size: Up to 1 in (2.5 cm)
Distribution: Found throughout North America

Freshwater Shrimp
(Order: Decapoda)

Freshwater shrimps resemble the sand hoppers and beach fleas found on the seashore. They are flattened sideways and curved into the shape of an arch. There are several different species, which vary in color from gray to greenish or orange-brown. You will not find them in stagnant ponds, but they are common in almost any clean, running water and in large lakes. Fish love to eat them, so these shrimp hide under stones and among plants. They eat decaying plants and animals.

Group: Amphipods
Size: Up to 1 in (2.5 cm)
Distribution: Eastern U.S.

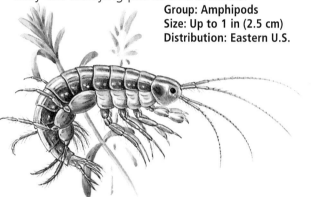

Eastern Crayfish
(*Cambarus bartonii*)

There are many different species of crayfish found throughout North America. They are easy to recognize because they look like miniature lobsters. However, it is very difficult to tell one species from another. The eastern crayfish is brown in color and has a smooth shell. Like other crayfish, it has five pairs of legs. The front pair are shaped as large pincers, which the crayfish use to capture prey. Crayfish make a tasty meal for fish, birds, turtles, otters— and humans!

Group: Crayfishes
Size: 2–6 in (5–15 cm)
Distribution: Eastern U.S.

Pearl Mussel
(Family: Margaritiferidae)

Pearl mussels live on the sandy bottoms of cool, clear streams and small rivers. Their thick, heavy shells are yellow-brown when young, changing to dark brown or black as the animal ages. Inside, the shell is pearly-white. Sometimes the pearl mussel forms small pearls. Like some other mussels, the newly hatched young attach themselves to fish and feed off them for a few weeks. These mussels grow very slowly and can live to be 90 years old!

Group: Pearly mussels
Size: 3–6 in (7.5–15 cm)
Distribution: Eastern pearl mussel on the Atlantic coast of Canada and the U.S.; western pearl mussel on the Pacific coast of Canada and the U.S.

Keep Them at Home

It's easy to make your own temporary aquarium using water and animals from a pond. Keeping the aquarium at home will let you study your specimens every day and chart their progress. Use this book to help you identify the animals you find and make a list of them. Repeat this at regular intervals. You may find that new animals have "magically" appeared. They have hatched out of tiny eggs or changed from larvae into adults.

Check with your teacher or an expert at a nature center before collecting animals for these activities. The teacher or expert may instead recommend a different activity that will be more appropriate for your locality. Collecting animals from the wild can be harmful to animals or their environment, or to you, so it always is best to get expert advice and to have an adult along on any expedition.

Make an aquarium

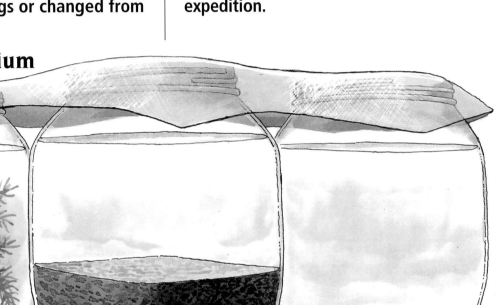

1 **Buy three cheap plastic aquariums** at your local pet store, or else use large jars. If you use jars, they must have wide openings to allow in plenty of air. Wash and rinse the containers well.
2 **Half-fill the first container with pond weed** and then fill it with pond water.
3 **In the second container, place a good layer of mud,** taken from the bottom of the pond, and then fill the rest of the container with pond water.
4 **Fill the third container with pond water only.** Put the containers outside in the shade, and cover them with netting. (**This is a warm-weather experiment.**)
5 **Look into the containers after a day** to see what has crawled out of the weeds and mud. Find out which of your containers has the widest variety of animals.
6 **Your aquariums should last for several weeks,** provided they are kept cool and there is a large enough surface of water in contact with the air.

Caddis cases

If you find caddisfly cases with the larvae still in them, you can watch how they build their home. Each caddis case is open at both ends to allow a flow of water through it.

1 **If you push a matchstick very gently into the narrow end of the case,** the caddisfly larva will come out, as it does not like being tickled! Now you can see it clearly. It will go back inside given the chance.

2 **Take away its old case** and keep the larva in a plastic box or jar in a cool, shady place. Fill the jar or box with the pond water in which you found the larva.
3 **Put in some tiny colored beads,** and the larva will rebuild its home out of these.

4 **Or you can give it pieces of the material** it normally uses, such as twigs or shells, and watch it rebuild its home from these items.
5 **It's best to try this experiment with several caddisfly larvae,** in case one of them is uncooperative.

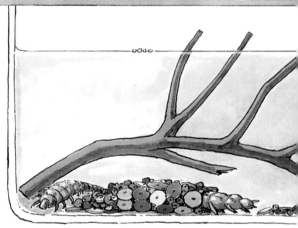

The somersaulting hydra

A hydra is a small animal that is up to about 1/2 inch (13 mm) long when expanded (see page 40). It looks like a hollow tube with a ring of tentacles at one end surrounding the mouth, and it can move slowly by turning somersaults!

1 **Find a pond or ditch where there is a carpet of duckweed** on the surface, or many floating water-lily leaves.

2 **Collect water-lily leaves** and look on the underside for blobs that look like jelly.
3 **Lift off these blobs with a paintbrush,** and put them in pond water in a jar. If they are hydra, they will soon expand.
4 **Collect a quantity of duckweed** and put it into a large jar of pond water. Keep it until the next day. Look at the sides of the jar for hydra. Watch them. They might somersault for you.

Slow Rivers & Canals

Where a river or stream reaches flat ground, its waters spread out and slow down. Mud and sand carried by the water settle and make a soft, muddy bottom in which many plants are able to grow. Water lilies, reeds, and sedges provide shelter for amphibians. Hiding on the bottom and among the weeds in the warm, murky water are freshwater shrimps, mollusks, snails, and crayfish.

Not all slow-moving rivers are muddy, however. While lowland rivers are usually murky, rivers flowing through chalk areas are often crystal clear. Water snails, crayfish, and shrimps thrive in these lime-rich waters, as do a wide variety of fish. This picture shows some animals from this book—see how many you can identify.

Mud Salamander
(Pseudotriton montanus)

Muddy springs and streams are the favorite habitats of this salamander, as its name suggests. The mud salamander is easy to spot because it is colored coral-pink, bright red, or a brownish salmon-pink. It has scattered black spots, and its belly is reddish or yellowish. Look in mucky areas by streamsides for this creature, but move quietly, as it may burrow into the mud when it hears you coming! If you find a salamander like this in a clear stream, it may be a red salamander (see page 59).

Group: Lungless salamanders
Size: 3–8 in (7.5–20 cm)
Distribution: Eastern coastal areas of the U.S.

Pickerel Frog
(Rana palustris)

This small, smooth-skinned frog has two parallel rows of square-shaped spots running down its back. The body is tan and the spots are darker. A good way to recognize this frog is by the bright yellow or orange marks under its hind legs and by its whitish belly. The pickerel frog has a steady, low-pitched croak. It comes out mainly at night and can produce a nasty liquid from its skin that causes predators such as snakes to avoid it. **Caution: This liquid can irritate your skin if you touch a pickerel frog.**

Group: Tree frogs
Size: 2–3½ in (5–9 cm)
Distribution: Throughout most of the eastern U.S.

Dwarf Waterdog
(Necturus punctatus)

Group: Mud puppies and waterdogs
Size: 4–8 in (10–20 cm)
Distribution: Southeastern coastal areas of the U.S.

This little salamander is like the mud puppy, or waterdog, on page 12, but it is much smaller. It is dark brown or grayish-black, with no patterns or markings at all. Its belly is gray, and bushy gills are visible by its neck. There are four toes on each of its feet. The dwarf waterdog prefers to live in slow, muddy-bottomed streams.

Reptiles

Slow Rivers & Canals

Smooth Softshell Turtle
(Apalone mutica)

As the name suggests, instead of a hard shell, this softshell turtle has a completely smooth skin on its back, with no lumps, bumps, or spines. Its skin is olive to orange-brown, with various patterns of dots, dashes, or blotches. The females are larger than the males and may have a mottled pattern on their backs. This turtle lives in rivers and large streams with sandy or muddy bottoms.

It spends most of its time in the water, feeding on crayfish, frogs, and fish. At times it sunbathes on sandbanks, but it will quickly dive back into the water if approached.

Group: Softshell turtles
Size: Males 4½–7 in (11.5–18 cm); females 7–14 in (18–35 cm)
Distribution: Central U.S.

Common Musk Turtle
(Sternotherus odoratus)

Other names for this small turtle are stinkpot turtle and stinking jim, because it gives out a very smelly liquid if disturbed. Its shell is smooth, with a high dome, and is olive-brown in color. There are two yellow stripes on either side of its head. Its undershell is small, with a lot of exposed flesh between its scales. The common musk turtle lives in slow-flowing, shallow waters that have muddy bottoms. It spends most of its time feeding on plants and decaying animals at the bottom of the water. Sometimes it basks on overhanging trees and shrubs, but it will drop back into the water if frightened. **Be careful with this turtle, as males are very aggressive and can give a nasty bite.**
Group: Musk and mud turtles—Size: 3–5 in (7.5–12.5 cm)
Distribution: Southeastern Canada and most of the eastern U.S.

Spiny Softshell
(Apalone spinifera)

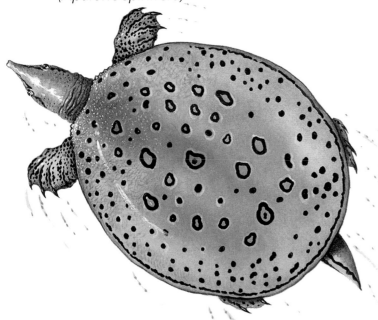

Like all softshells, this turtle has soft, leathery skin. It features a long neck and a tubelike snout. It is olive or tan in color, often with black-edged spots or dark mottling. There are spiny bumps on the front of the shell and sometimes over the back as well. The spiny softshell often lives in rivers, but it also likes creeks, ponds, and lakes. You may find it hard to spot a spiny softshell—it moves fast on land, and also in water (where it chases minnows and other prey). Softshells also like to sunbathe on banks and logs. **Be careful of this turtle, as it can give a nasty bite, and it scratches too.**
Group: Softshell turtles
Size: Males 5–9 in (12.5–23 cm); females 6–18 in (15–45.5 cm)
Distribution: Central and eastern U.S., with scattered populations elsewhere

Queen Snake
(Regina septemvittata)

This snake is medium in size and is colored olive-brown to dark brown. Its belly and sides are striped with yellow and brown. The queen snake lives near streams and small rivers that have rocky bottoms; it feeds almost entirely on crayfish. It often sunbathes on trees and shrubs overhanging the water—if disturbed, it drops into the water to hide. Females give birth to live young between July and September.
Group: Colubrid snakes
Size: 1¼–3 ft (0.3–0.9 m)
Distribution: Central, southern, and eastern U.S.

Yellow Mud Turtle
(Kinosternon flavescens)

The yellow mud turtle gets its name from its yellow undershell and its yellow jaw and throat. Its top shell is olive to brown. It lives in slow-moving waters with muddy or sandy bottoms, and it feeds on worms, crustaceans, snails, and tadpoles. It comes out to hunt on land at dawn or dusk. This turtle buries itself under leaves or in mud under the water and hibernates in the winter.
Group: Musk and mud turtles
Size: 3½–7 in (9–18 cm)
Distribution: Central and southern U.S., and some in the southwestern U.S.

Eastern Mud Turtle
(Kinosternon subrubrum)

This turtle has an oblong, smooth shell, colored olive to dark brown. The undershell is yellow to brown. The head is usually dark brown with pale streaks or spots. Look for the mud turtle in shallow, slow-moving water where there are plenty of weeds. It spends most of its time on the muddy bottom, but it often travels over land during the summer. At this time, you may see it slowly crossing a road—sadly, many mud turtles are killed by cars. If its habitat dries up, the mud turtle can burrow into the mud and survive there until the rains replenish the waters.
Group: Musk and mud turtles
Size: 3–5 in (7.5–12.5 cm)
Distribution: Eastern, southern, and central U.S.

Stonecat
(Noturus flavus)

This catfish is mostly brownish-gray, with a white belly, chin, and barbels ("whiskers"). Its snout hangs slightly over its lower jaw. The stonecat lives in streams or slow-moving rivers that flow over gravel. It feeds on water insects on the bottom, as well as small fish, snails, and crustaceans. It spends most of the day hidden under a rock and comes out at night to feed. **Be careful with this kind of catfish, as it has poisonous spines on the fins behind the gill cover.**

Group: Catfishes
Size: Up to 12 in (30 cm)
Distribution: Central Canada and most of the northern central U.S.

Iowa Darter
(Etheostoma exile)

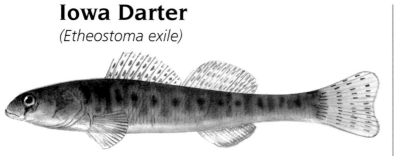

This fish has a slender body covered in medium-sized scales. It is olive-brown in color, with several dark red blotches on its sides. There are two fins on its back, and the first one has 8 to 10 spines. The tail fin is rounded with black spots. The Iowa darter lives in quiet areas of streams where plants grow and lakes with mud and sand bottoms. It feeds on insects, small crustaceans, and snails.

Group: Darters and perches
Size: Up to 3 in (7.5 cm)
Distribution: Eastern and central Canada, and north in the eastern and central U.S.

Mosquito Fish
(Gambusia spp.)

This small fish has a stout, pale-colored body covered with noticeable scales outlined in black. There are black spots on its sides, and on its single back fin and rounded tail fin. It has a small head with an upturned mouth, which it uses to snatch insects from the water surface. It gets the name mosquito fish from its preferred diet of mosquito larvae. You may see this fish in swamps, ditches, ponds, lakes, and slow-moving streams. The females do not lay eggs but instead give birth to live young.

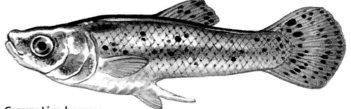

Group: Live bearers
Size: 2–3 in (5–7.5 cm)
Distribution: Eastern and central U.S.

Asiatic Clam
(Corbicula fluminea)

Also called the little basket clam, this bivalve lives in rivers, canals, and lakes. Its shell is brown with a blackish coating on the outside and purple or blue on the inside. It is almost triangular in shape. Like mussels, the clam feeds by taking in water from which it filters out food. It then ejects the waste water. It uses two siphon tubes for this purpose. It often takes over a stream and can be present in incredible numbers.
Group: Basket clams—Size: 1–2½ in (2.5–6.5 cm)
Distribution: Introduced from Southeast Asia, now found in most of the southern and central U.S.

Freshwater Limpet
(Ferrissia spp.)

Like the limpets you find on the seashore, freshwater limpets live firmly attached to rocks, mussel shells, stones, or plants. They can move about grazing on vegetation, but will clamp down firmly on a plant or stone if threatened. The shell is cone-shaped, with a curved-back top. Some of these limpets like the still water of ponds and lakes, while others prefer streams and rivers. River-dwelling limpets have tougher shells to withstand the flow of water.
Group: Freshwater limpets
Size: Up to ½ in (1 cm)
Distribution: Found across North America

River Snail
(Viviparus viviparus)

The shell of the river snail is thick and patterned, with a big, D-shaped opening. The shell may be patterned with zigzag lines or can be plain. It lives mostly in running waters, such as streams and rivers, but it may also be seen in canals and ponds. When the snail retreats into its shell, it seals the opening with a "lid" called an operculum.
Group: River snails—Size: Up to ¾ in (2 cm)
Distribution: Found across North America

Freshwater Mussel
(Class: Bivalvia)

Freshwater mussels live in ponds, canals, rivers, and streams. They filter their food from the water, as they lie half-buried in the mud. Many types of mussels live in fresh water, and it can be difficult to tell them apart. The outer shell of a freshwater mussel can be one of many different colors, but the inside shells are usually an iridescent mother-of-pearl. This pearly inner shell has led to the over-harvesting of freshwater mussels in the United States, as for years the shells were used in the button industry.
Group: Freshwater mussels
Size: Up to 6 in (15 cm)
Distribution: Found across North America

Find Out More

Glossary

amphibian: type of cold-blooded animal that was the first vertebrate (animal with a backbone) to spend part of its life on land (unlike fish, which spend all their lives underwater); amphibians lay their eggs in water and the young start life there, breathing through gills; amphibians then usually develop into an adult form, using lungs to breathe and living on land

barbels: "whiskers" on the chins of members of the catfish family

crustacean: soft-bodied animal without a backbone; crustaceans have a hard outer shell, long feelers, and many pairs of jointed legs

deciduous: tree that loses its leaves in the fall; most broadleaf trees are deciduous

eft: young stage of a salamander or newt

fish: cold-blooded animal with a backbone and fins; fish live all their lives underwater, breathing through gills

frog: amphibian that typically has webbed feet, long, powerful hind legs, and smooth skin; the young stage is called a tadpole

habitat: environment (area) that is the natural home of certain plants and animals

hibernate: to spend either a whole season or a period of severe weather in a state of deep sleep, especially one marked by a distinct lowering of metabolism rate and body temperature

mollusk: soft-bodied animal without a backbone; most mollusks, such as snails and clams, have shells

newt: member of the salamander group; the young stage is called an eft

nymph: young stage of certain winged insects, such as grasshoppers; nymphs that live underwater, such as those of mayflies and dragonflies, are usually called naiads

operculum: horny plate that some mollusks use to seal the entrance to their shells

predator: carnivorous (meat-eating) animal that eats mostly other animals

reptile: cold-blooded animal with a backbone; unlike amphibians, reptiles can spend all their lives on land, though some live in water

salamander: amphibian that has a tail, four legs, and soft, moist skin; the young stage is called an eft

snake: reptile that has an extended body, a tapering tail, no legs, and scaly skin

tadpole: young stage of a frog or toad

toad: amphibian that typically has webbed feet, long, powerful hind legs, and rough, warty skin; the young stage is called a tadpole

turtle: reptile that has a toothless beak, a soft body, four legs, and a tough shell

Organizations

The **American Society of Ichthyologists and Herpetologists** is a group for professional zoologists and serious amateurs. (Ichthyology is the study of fish; herpetology is the study of reptiles). Contact: American Society of Ichthyologists and Herpetologists, Department of Biological Sciences, Florida International University, North Miami, Florida 33181, (305) 919-5651. http://www.asih.org

In Canada, the **Canadian Nature Federation** is a good starting point for information about freshwater animals. Contact: Canadian Nature Federation, Suite 606, 1 Nicholas Street, Ottawa, Ontario K1N 7B7; (800) 267-4088. http://www.cnf.ca

The **North American Native Fishes Association** is interested in studying and conserving American fish. Write to: North American Native Fishes Association, 1107 Argonne Drive, Baltimore, Maryland 21218. http://www.nanfa.org

Reptile and Amphibian Magazine is published every second month. To subscribe to it, write to: *Reptile and Amphibian Magazine*, RD# 3, Box 3709–A, Pottsville, Pennsylvania 17901.

The **Society for the Study of Amphibians and Reptiles** is a good group from which to gather information about freshwater animals. Contact: Society for the Study of Amphibians and Reptiles, P.O. Box 253, Marceline, Missouri 64658-0253; (660) 256-3252. http://www.ssarherps.org

Index

Additional Resources

The Encyclopedia of Aquatic Life Keith Banister and Andrew Campbell (Facts on File, 1985).

A Field Guide to Freshwater Fishes Lawrence M. Page and Brooks M. Burr (Houghton Mifflin, 1991).

Firefly Encyclopedia of Insects and Spiders Christopher O'Toole, editor (Firefly Books, 2002).

Fresh-Water Invertebrates of the United States Robert W. Pennak (Wiley, 1978).

National Audubon Society Field Guide to Fishes: North America Carter Rowell Gilbert and James D. Williams (Knopf, 2002).

National Audubon Society Field Guide to North American Insects and Spiders Lorus and Margery Milne (Knopf, 2003).

Snakes: The Evolution of Mystery in Nature Harry W. Greene (University of California Press, 1997).

Index

See *World Book's Science & Nature Guides Resources & Cumulative Index* volume for an explanation of the system used by scientists to classify living things.